A Jann Plan
Creative Origins Advocacy Teach Peace and Creative Accountability

by

Gregg K. Jann

RoseDog Books
PITTSBURGH, PENNSYLVANIA 15222

RoseDog Books
701 Smithfield Street
Pittsburgh, PA 15222
Visit our website at *www.rosedogbookstore.com*

ISBN: 978-1-4809-1722-4
eISBN: 978-1-4809-1723-1

Table of Contents

Administrative/Reverse Usury for Money to Origin Design
Personal Note

Starting Poem

I am
To Do This-
A Better Life for Me!
With joy to my entire family and,
To honor the reforms I participated in,
for I felt thoughts in my wall outward were hidden.
I was a lot "unable-sorry" keeping me from wife, my relationship just wished for.
With engagement beyond hope, want for actualizing so I love what's in store
the rest of the way.
Author

Introduction

Customer Service/Hold Economy

Spoken in process and written 5/30/2013 by Gregg K. Jann

Customer Service staff can change the direction of their energy in positive manner away from themselves to listen to the other person's side and even lose company money in the short run. In the long run a better emotion is kept with the irate or simply disappointed customer who formerly worked up steam to organize a complaint, gather receipts in a shopping bag, and judge herself to be talented in determining appropriate policy toward her without personalization. The Occupy Wall Street movement in my town lives rough and talks of the 99% in both justice and who is the bully. A change to them and for business practices is to work another direction, toward the person point of a colleague or the customer base. Keeping personal boundaries is necessary to maintain selfhood and be a strong human as he focuses on the needs kindly of the consumer. Keep in heart and mind the authenticity is more in our capitalist economy to keep in spirit with our humanity and the adjoining transaction which is the service point, not the ownership.

A "hold for" economy is where the process maintains integrity with the origin as service point. A person, she could be weakened by emotions or disability, is not cheated from her reward of her creations and properties. Trusts are needed, and the only reform we may have done outside of illegalizing them during Clinton's era is not to have Blind Trusts whereby the recipient doesn't know of the trust or how to get at it. Trusts still are truthfully set up by others. Is this existence of a trust a question for the Internet and other famous inventions we have had since the "Tear Down This Wall" speech eloquently spoken in Europe by Reagan? What do we do with Presidential examples used in anecdotes and speeches and productive gain of the country, and can we do better with our beloved contributors with a Customer Service/Hold economy?

Chapter 1

Repast and Recollection Entries to Gain Skill

Blog entries since Book I, credited Counseling Essays

Acne from Important Food Stolen, Similar
Sun, 2013-05-19 20:07

- <u>Prevention and Health</u>

A doctor saying the cause of your disease is "natural consequences" means behavioral. Unhealthy lifestyles leading challenges cause judgment on our mind's functions and controls. There's stuff just not liked by medicine who are MD's. These "natural consequences" can emanate from community input and patient reports appearing to work as out of court convictions from non-lovers who punish.

Take acne. When someone says she has it from eating too much chocolate, consider if the chocolate was a romance gift for her father to give and a 2nd time if the chocolate was a love offering from a church/family friend to her mother. Stealing the protein-laden meat from a teenage football player by a brother soon zit full is further evidence of Medicine putting in their 2 cents too dirty.

Family supports may be saturated with harm, with doctors siding for out-going personality playing favorites in blame games. The usual family forensics of mental illness can hide poison slipped for too "cute" behavior of the person now disabled for life.

Edited: Too cute like a yellow [truck company] baseball cap for selling the most newspapers for a non-New York Times newspaper and wearing it on a bicoastal visit with his Dad, both with brother seated almost directly and low behind home plate at Yankee stadium which was a surprise, unexpected event that day. He was 14 this trip, first and one of many to visit his father. The father worked across Columbia University at the Interfaith Center on Riverside Dr, when he wasn't a Presbyterian Minister Sundays in New York and throughout the nation. One visit from San Francisco during college years Gregg fled back NY home there at his office commute after not completely re-membering a Subway ride that was re-enacted on TV as a runaway train acci-dent about a year ago. Was the jet airplane the Concorde that Gregg flew in on the return flight this same particular trip with details always hazy? Gregg also had a "scholarship" to watch University of California Golden Bear foot-ball games with Mother during and after an award winning year on a cham-pionship Pop Warner football team.

Can we assume criminal slander to steal from a "tall" success by people using medicine wrongly or did he recover as target source designer of psy-chotropic meds with goodness to his core? The dedication presented for A Jann Plan: Creative Origins Advocacy is men of "ideas with merit" that a State Assembly staffer recognized the author to have versus the legal quid-pro-quo of political fundraising in blocking and un-crediting the sources of legislation and for profit endeavors like the Entertainment business.

Aging Family Supports Become Normal
Wed, 2013-05-15 00:08

- Family and Friends

Family visiting doesn't go away with adulthood. Staying at home living with a parent or so longer can encourage the closeness both generations of family member may need. The disabled being like a coach in presence and pro-viding even just a warm body to a lump on the couch up to the elders' old age is not often praised but felt gratefully by most all in the family. We take our part, and the too young a person with a disability can do good adding in family senior years by always having been around.

The dependent elder as a young softie may need a bolt of lightning to get out of here to finish life like my dad did. He was a role model in ways, by re-marrying at 57 him, her younger than him by over 20 years. He shows I still have life ahead at mid-century. I want to carry better care toward others to define I'm strong for relationship. It is normally family needing quality to keep having times together from more than one state away.

Creative Process from Inside Own Mind
Wed, 2013-04-24 12:42

- Prevention and Health

Having Coach I marketing on my business card, and Counselor within my experience on my resume, succeeding in my victorious elections and published writing in whatever field or endeavor I find myself does not mean I collaborate well with everybody. At least I don't steal from others at all. My contemplation seems un-fun and unfriendly compared to my heart expressed in writing or the work I do.

My creative process stems from a test in Management graduate training at an Extended University classroom that classified me as a "creative type." This is opposed to downright creative or, for example a "results oriented" executive. The process of a hard background TV Guide told me as a youth were invaluable to American comic stock. Thugs beat them or threatened them as the source target came up with humor and sketches. I have not had an easy life since of just banquets and board meetings, and suffered fools and dirty politics where I earned a job.

My humor is to myself to keep mood in check for the most part. I struggle and fight back nicely at the environment blocking, ignoring, and taking from me in my wallet. Sometimes I have such an Exoshell keeping myself pure that I respond to internal stimuli later while I make things up in fantasy and limerance love style to "a women." A fun delusional symptom is my giggling to myself out of order is more to writers. It means I can see my hobby of hiking in wilderness with a failed biker/musician friend and trying not to tell him I was thinking of girls I liked back while a happy youth, or see a bright empty red room like my mother's womb just last week, or emotionally being forced into success at some point where I have a healthy reluctance from attention.

Explanation: Limerance are a love style to one phantom by a heartful of a person, which can be real in person just needing to land to be down to earth after daydreaming about her. Toward a star in media is a relatable lust, but for Limerance the love is present like ordinary adults. Deep imagination stricken hurt to make an obsession with someone's present love is a Greek tragedy and do you hear laughing? I nursed limerance love to a work neighbor 1 mile away and was faithful while having healthy fantasies with a normal rotation of beautiful women. A work unionization struggle cost me that women's life, even just to get in a dating relationship with whom I loved. Or was it no money to afford a wife that I wanted that the system and employers blocked with? Was the counselor and program manager I was strangled by Supervisor to keep away from experiencing this young love an actual body double program of replacement players meant to rate insanity or disability of a Capgrass (-priest) abuse? Nice Guys Finish Last in Time is my belief about Fuck Planet and A-hole people toward the Exoshell who could have sang BF lyrics and tunes not gay.

Update: A creative process making a person too quiet so he would pass anonymous sound mind tests in not revealing weird phenomena can be presented when safe and health care does no more harm to the person's stability and does not block his wishes to reach standing as a realization. A filling-in of loose ends in awareness gaps in events where happenings and occurrences are registered in subconscious but a nawing of agitation calmly or more pronounced is at the back of the mind. Here something in the memory gap took place experienced not in awareness, which can be added in quality where a lapse of consciousness is replaced with imagination and made up stories. Positive visioning or useful to the moment memories false or in repast are then woven into a reality either true in actuality or described as good fiction. RE: Recollection and Repast - Did the originations of Book II really emanate with truth as written here, and if so how did the author's products of his mind spread with the various entities recognizing the work as worth utilization but not giving the man who lead the ideas his credit on the IP worth value?

Encounter: She was more than one beautiful woman the phantom was in unknowns, and he didn't see visually she was multiples until sending printing to the copyright office this Book II. (False to his senses is that Capgras Syndrome is the paranoia about many people taking one person's place in a Sherlock Holmes style investigation sense for not accepting Body Doubles of different people thought of as just one. To discount paranoia's role in this case, BD's are implemented in Hollywood state for why we don't always know. Union fight to disqualify an old man may be one reason. We can't underestimate the unethical conduct of the MH System. He saw things transposing images while head strong in love and defensive in high anxiety being made something he never knew he was.) For his reality, he was waiting for her to marry while he blushed up feeling in love and sheer ecstasy each month for training meeting when she passed by in his darkness of illness. His strategy of using too much finesse did get hit for women protesting in the here and now among beautiful acquaintances, but his prayers for one double chastity woman for relationship to marry weren't answered neither was spouse within reach afterward to find. Old Man in Love and he did get young beautiful women in force meat on him that he didn't initiate contact nor did he do the sissy fighting that one lawyer would have liked as he was always the decent one. Funny how good moral character works on getting younger and more beautiful women, but sterling character was taken advantage of in a tarnishing experience of sullying the "charged-Capgras target," hero in mental health over years that he still is not sure of ever happening except for physical evidence he didn't know would show that way.

Furtherance: The other end of his creativity is self denial of the common culture in process to not fit the same mold as the rest in imagination, mainly for his youth and college eras before enough rules and social structure were to be given to one young at heart man. Just thinking of the fun and hearing spotty reviews is lonely away from emotional connection of friends. And a lot of un-support for a decent male in lands of few other than Republicans and outlaws back hometown, whose background to him chose not to talk with one quiet person who listened to the stereo music of rock and roll. He did share verbally wherever he found togetherness, including classrooms in many schools and we know in printed words all his adult life. The later years' hard knocks of history-making in emotional toil or the difficulty of head banging processes and contending with the jealousies of man can be seen as life enhancing by the beholder/creator in landing interpersonally, for no longer "spacing out" in day dreams or not visioning without experience.

The women unseen were taking advantage from a time a young boyhood talking politics and religion in America before the women arrived, which wrongly can be punished by rival organized Church of One Kind to a different type of ambition. Surprising with insight and innovation on the problems of the day from when he was 5 years old and onward up to running for election as a peace candidate imparting peace skills to young students nearing the launch of making the <u>The 40 Year Old Virgin</u>.

For advice to reader is to know that bad people un-money those few who are making a difference in the world and in people's lives who are innocently, perhaps naively, made poor. The hard line status quo of these "Structurists" forcing down on creative influences use money and a self serving God to show who is boss, and contain the spread of wordsmiths using threats of no talent for not matching significance as widespread cultural impact needs a source. Status quo of banks and lawyers and many organizational officials say not to credit or even thank sources.

My business plan/ballot proposal in this book shall assist us with true beginnings credits for a more honest, changed capitalism to go along with a kinder, gentler nation that is authentic to people of any generation. Struggle I have done. "Charge On" worth US Diplomatic Corps is a quote from Jim Wilkinson while at a general dinner meeting of the Santa Rosa Democratic Club to me personally that I shall keep true, more, and in my heart for better rightness with outward example best we can.

A "You" Person, "Health Secrecy," and International Trade Deals
Mon, 2013-04-08 11:42

- <u>Critical Thinking Fighting Suppression</u>

Flashes of brilliant "blurting out" of creativity that changed the society we abide to seem indecipherable because of "health secrecy" we need. Bucking the Mental Health System for their money and transformation in a popular tax ballot using a counselor's effort, his own governance both liaison and elected, and spiritual salesmanship of Jann DA are not meaningless to a thoughtful man in his heart, mind and soul.

People only caring for themselves and their relational accounts can hurt the economy and bond ratings by not paying or even acknowledging the policy participant and guide who wants an honestly large credit and income. Can't we say this about the internet too?

If Governor, President, CEO, or just Church Member, how hard a weakness is our usury and theft on first, originals, and uniqueness for products, services, and processes that mean commercial applications from idealism for international vibrancy since before the days the Berlin Wall fell.

Credit: I saw printed in a health article the word "indecipherable" in the LA Times soon after this blog entry was posted. Unique word in context like that shows I was read by journalism and health researchers before the public. I started writing in college and felt like I was more read by the public than my private research assignment and wrote more words to be read than words to professor. Now we do health prescriptions worth business. My Google Analytics page doesn't show LA reading my blog like they're supposed to, so someone North is talented with me and I wish I knew who.

Giants Pitcher's Nicknames of 70s and 80s
Thu, 2013-03-21 21:52

* Reviews and Entertainment

It is just Too Asshole to talk to the County Patient Rights Advocate about his funding through my tax ballot design for what he said. I want Original Source Point recognized and economically rewarded for business and writers and policy participants, as a political issue to reform inauthentic enterprise and encourage creativity and rightful innovation. The PRA said to the consumer formerly appointed and elected officer that this was "self aggrandizing" and it meant "look at me" like the disco dance era for snotty kids. The bureaucrat encourages dishonesty in government and this Marquis Who's Who businessman, counselor, and school board member keeps trying to put together the money at the end of the day for vastly used ideas that fund the world we live in. "Read More" for ongoing EBU Original Source Point research for the summer.

It's hard to respect memory of long ago or of youth and very likeable if reputation is correct and accurate with due diligence. Let's try together to work on Original Source Point of Giants pitchers nicknames when I lived with my family as a youth for the spirit we need. Email me on the Contact Us page on Jannda.com and we will get to the rightful namer like I try to do as a wordsmith owner. It may be worth another Giants World Series Victory if we can get an honest bottom of Nicknames from my family and friends and the community out there.

John "The Count" Montefusco is a name I know I said to brother "https:/" and then I denied it to his face in a move after he asked me days later. He was a radial 60s older sibling threatened with a draft card a couple of years prior. I inherited naturally being a minister's son felt strongly and even then wanted to reform land about America's taking of first and original talent and products of my mind. John is a no-hit pitcher whose first major league at bat was a home run in 1974. My days were in the doldrums and The Count by Lon Simmons was my single most exciting radio experience. The Count of Monte Crisco is a make-up from our days as a youth.

"Bug"'s first pitch to my brother "Blockbuster" when I was 5 or 7 years old was a drop fork ball. Dad may have said a nickname for pitchers to me or to my brothers before or after I did. MY father was soon nationally known moving across the country to Manhattan. My oldest brother could play astronomy well enough for Cal as an astounding physics major and my catcher batted over .600 as a 12 year old in Little League playing third base and now homes a home on a hillside in Washington.

I may be all of these nicknames if memory is served correctly. From fun in a private grassy yard to responding to what I'm viewing with comments while having fun or studying, it's hard to know the process of communication to the radio announcer with the approval of player agents. Wikipedia.com reports the following pitchers, and we need to respect privacy. I am a firm protector of childhoods and currently feel some linkage from my creative products.

It looks like my aware to me "first" if specific instance and person captured or not was in 1974 or 1975. Who does the San Francisco G.M. give credit to for these pitchers fun moniker at the source of the nickname:

"The Count"

Ed "no hit" Halicki - is that a real name?

Greg "Moon Man" Minton - for his image and late night reliever duties. Wasn't that forwarded from my 1982 Chico days and fun talk about the dorm residents and Governor Brown, or if could have been from the sandlots of Peanuts ball we played here in Santa Rosa.

"Big Daddy" Reuschel - an experienced good pitcher on the team and we say those things.

Did our vanquished of 2012 in Detroit track down the origins of Mark "The Bird" Fydrich more publicly than the City by the Bay?

"Fear the Beard" of great fun of 2010 and "The Freak" and all of the above show how common the great game of baseball can be when city and team make a storied history.

Stories with fun names of respect are colorful and provide a lesson to be more than money without un-money to people who create our heritage through talent.

Using Tax Forms Only Payment of +/- Taxes
Wed, 2013-03-06 13:27

- Property Rights and Ethics

City business taxes and County business property assessments are not the only work product fees I pay. Fee-for-service items like a County parks pass to park not on a highway space for self and mother is an end or beginning of extra tax payments of activity. Using an online tax preparer software package for those rate payers on Social Security of some kind and earning less than $25,000 (make sure) is sometimes merely a record keeping good thing to do. Perhaps a state or federal tax return may be found to be unnecessary after filling out the online tax form and no personal income tax is due for that file. There can be only pay the tax preparation service making an activity based accounting enhancement that is unaffordable for too low an income to pay taxes or to make a worthwhile credit. What this country needs is a tax credit that means the electronic filing efficiency does not cost money just to file when that particular form does not have enough to go by to tax any money at all.

Parents of Adult Children to Keep Nurturing
Tue, 2013-02-19 14:42

- <u>Family and Friends</u>

The goal of a good parent through the difficult times of their off-springs' youth is to keep repeating to the child, "It's good to be adult friends with parents and children." The positive, nice words and emotional nurturing from above do not go away with a more equal partnership between young and old. This is especially true for people with disabilities. The younger person, no matter how difficult he/she felt he was in personality or in the upbringing methods he went through, should bear in mind at all times that a positive relationship with parents is great for happiness at adulthood. A mature relationship is best felt when family is on speaking terms and in cordial, warm relations throughout the family.

A disabled person is often more needy and needs help where normally healthy family members do not. A double, triple, up to near infinite doses of positive expectations to and from the person with a disability means bearing with him together.

Note: My Methodist membership, which is the church I belong and I presently attend a Presbyterian Men's Bible study, is considering adding "care" in the place of "love" mentioned again on a document professing faith. With the proposed Living Covenant, I now articulate better in church relationships emotional support is needed by family, along with housing and food. If family can't provide this then another legal body like church or school can implement hands on tools and some results for both young and old.

Kindness Leader Loves Through Policy
Fri, 2013-02-15 15:00

- Advocacy

We can look at 2 way relationships like the Ancient Greeks. Playful (Ludus), Companion, and Altruistic love styles are among the six known by the Greeks taught to us. A Love Style not mentioned is the author's Love through Policy - Caring for Many, and I also have provided economically for my charges. Children are affected by more complete character education soft skills taught that I wrote and talked about as a Governing Board member. Counselors and consumers are impacted by my firsthand leadership and founding union negotiations and struggles for more employment rights. A whole health industry is infused by my tax policy with resulting transformation by my design, strategy, and which passed in a ballot initiative. There was no thank you to me, no acknowledgments by management, no income reward for my talent I made to work for the people from public government bureaucrats. The Peace Guru with a Courtroom Judge's title of The Honorable is none other than Virgin de la Santa Rosa!!!

Permaculture Adds People to Earth Principle
Wed, 2013-02-06 19:38

- Holistic Community and Perma culture

Permaculture carries principles for humanity's best cooperation with the physical space we have on earth. I like to think an abundance of soft kindness throughout the social fabric is part of the process. Consider your environmental impact on earth. Keep present with us while doing your favorite spring time activity, from gardening to cleaning solvents for chores and transportation use.

Low carbon footprint calculated on fossil fuel emissions/consumption, recycling waste, and re-using manufactured goods for longer periods of time all make a more sustainable economy personally applied. Take a sustainable practices class or volunteer in the community and produce an increment of change. This helps each of our efforts to be green now and in the future to prevent destabilization of global alliances. We can help direct the economy to reach efficiency for including external variables like stemming the costs of pollution in dollars and for health of humans by respecting the ecosystem.

Titlist for New Movie Credits Listed on Film
Fri, 2013-01-18 18:26

- <u>Property Rights and Ethics</u>

Now is the season for awarding prizes for Hollywood movies. We suggest not an award so much, but new money from films to the people who create the title of a movie that connects well and gives direction while the title person guides the entire movie. I do know I am one feature length movie title, and have not received credit for the way I performed this task during my elected school board era. A second movie garnering attention in awards this year stirs up a reminding memory of a doctor's visit long ago. These movies are a decade apart in making, and I tell you stealing the movie name of the beginning decade of ten years ago can start wars and make peace when corrected. This reform of crediting the movie title to a person gets a more genuine Hollywood to inspire us as people, lets creative types into the scene locally and in the capital of entertainment, and builds more authenticity to counter our creativity and leadership problem here in California.

Another Claim: At this month, I visited the North Bay Recruiting Office of the US Army and provided a copy of my Pearl Harbor Remembrance Day writing. I spoke of the concepts about myself and the Peace Department. I told the Staff Sergeant "Joan Jett" that I came in to the all recruiting office in the Federal Building back in spring of 1986 and changed the name of "Harpo" which he said, to "Oprah Winfrey" which I said, which others may be more knowledgeable about in knowing what's what. I told them I get manipulated by the media in over-military that wasn't the true me, this visit in '86 because of a German bombing in a disco while dancing was a great hobby of mine. I did not further my Officer Candidate application in 1986, because I described I wanted to invent peer counseling which I determined was a need from a 60 Minutes Program on schizophrenia. The recommendations and signatures required seemed not like I was and that blocked along with assumed threats to a peacenik usually. I wanted to be a businessman, big time with my computers and peace input published previously. I told Ms Jett the AIDS name and acronym was first and originally spoken by me but I withheld saying so that 1986 Spring along with any health condition for which I was getting treatment. Now I'm feeling vastly influential and having some productive life registered in Marquis Who's Who of America. I may be one who is inventing a Peace Department with computer and military and rightful, authenticity in ownership credit, and this month's visit was a good one I continue to hope for with military buttress in my plans well for my money. And not butt toward. I'm not an enemy, just got taken advantage of while hurt pre-copy right.

Emotion Buttress for Change I Need
Wed, 2013-01-02 19:58

- Motivation

A New Year's Resolution is standard for a motivational goal to try to change a habit or gain new ground. An emotional bolster that wasn't there before or is felt stronger can begin the process of a personal transformation. Using this emotional buttress like a bookend holding fast the new behavior for the foreseeable future will give one the comfort and security needed at the heart of a new way of being. "Just wanting to change whenever I feel like it" can more easily revert to the same old behavior when the chips are down. A routine that changed with a startle or a strong hold can keep the adrenaline and excitement focused on the hard work of transitions. A steady, unknown progression with maybe a compliment is best. A firm start day like Jann. 1 added with emotional support is a winner. Time will tell.

My first cold weather family Holiday season in Washington state ending 2012 refreshing my desire to exercise can be attributed to family together and support with the New Year a strategic starting point. From long ago, I continue to learn from my first mini-desert rock formation vacation with my family and it set me up for some better teenage habits. I am hoping for the same invigoration to me on health and hygiene.

Reverse Usury for Sustainability
Thu, 2012-12-20 14:27

- Property Rights and Ethics

In the U.S. Constitution it says the government needs to pay for property it takes from people. Is there a problem with recognition of people and what they did? Introduction to Economics will educate students the factors of production are land, labor, and capital. Creative product comes from people. New credits for any person developing Intellectual Property is a good direction to lead for our country if the economy wants to be refreshed and made more authentic. [Count clients as people, which professional judgment deletes for easy money.]

Some elements we misjudge the source of the capitalist endeavor is the value of the Person, value of the Identity, and recognizing the Work Products wherever the contributor has been, including student years and from the home. Government wants to use sources, so does business - all without telling you nor paying you. What's one to do?

A Renewed Day Hopes the Peace Department
Fri, 2012-12-07 15:35

* Homeland into Foreign Policy

Peace is an interactive rigmarole with people, ideas, and resources - enough for emotional security; with kindness surroundings, feelings aimed for each inner me of persons; and good faith from every individual used with freedom even simplicity.

This day started World War II by a sneak attack invasion from Japan. We can say war is won on the home front. Improving our nation by adding to us care and support with taxes, treatment, and tips all during this war of retribution is a great achievement of the states. A Great American Medal of Honor for an individual goes beyond his condition to help dialog of his people. The author supplying an alias for stopping the FBI's Most Wanted terrorist while I was talking a newspaper over coffee with an ambassador showed up in the President's speech announcing a major blow to the Taliban in Pakistan.

We won the wars, with appreciation to the soldiers and those supporting them. Know the peace side stepped to the plate. Stop the sleight by ending harm and make whole victims of discrimination of these people of peace creed.

A Department of Peace needs to provide federal guidance and payment rules for progress and change for education, health and welfare, the work place, and source points and creative enterprise tips whereby all needing innovation for pay. For example, by applying stronger civil rights so that a person with disability can own and profit from intellectual property source points, from songs to legislation to Hollywood and even helping to invent the internet.

A Peace Department dedicated to changing past practices for the people, individuals, and movements, while rewarding the designer and target sources. We can reverse the ethics of not paying someone because they volunteered first, or enable hiring people who served our country for elections or in other ways, and employ people who are not liked by the workplace because they need to improve themselves as a service to them.

A federal department can assist the strong or unique service to change the systems to make something different, or to bolster the weak individuals to make contributions an individual or group needs; all permitting progress toward better quality or trying for a better fairness to one and all.

A Peace Department in Washington is better than a collection of local government offices who hear you. It's the federal treasury to pay talent and accomplishments for the rightful person who lead them or performed them, no matter who you are.

Cheers to recognize a Peace Department - for us, for money, to compare kindness, to make better, to like everyone here and abroad.

Grateful with Appreciation Includes Hope
Mon, 2012-11-19 13:15

- Prevention and Health

It spoils the effect of gratefulness to want more or better from life without the spirit of appreciation. A quality of hope fits importantly to the senses of thanking people, circumstances, and spirit. However meager to you or disappointing things feel to you, it is vital to appreciate what you have and what you are feeling. Health and wellness come from feeling better than you did when you felt bad, and that takes appreciation then and now. Motivation to keep processing and acting to end depression, or working for more productivity out of a malaise, can come from appreciating a bad lot in life. Hoping for better than now and keeping hold of a spiritual justice of rightness will maintain your good fight through your struggles for good present moments when recovery arrives.

President Agrees to Nation Building Us
Sat, 2012-10-27 12:40

- Homeland into Foreign Policy

Switching the TV channel during a Giants World Series game victory, I heard President Obama say midway through the debate: "We both believe in Nation Building - for our friends and other nations and in Nation Building within our own country." Community Building to me means cohesiveness and people getting along no matter what walk of life they traverse. The US Nation Building within our borders is best described by California's Mental Health Services Act designed by me and passed into law, which taxed millionaire incomes.

Adding a necessary medical field usually benefiting sub-populations of poor, undeserving, or plainly victims of injustice and taxing millionaires for fairness making more care to show for ourselves to present and in our heart of hearts for one another are 2 results. We implemented the citizens through a government process to help a weakness we have. In Sacramento planning meetings early in the process I verbally referred to my graduate training from Sonoma State on Maslow's Hierarchy of Needs and misquoted San Francisco Chronicle columnist Herb Caen from my teenage years in high school where he said a million dollars doesn't mean anything anymore. Caen was talking about the price of houses. I was using my Meaningful Psychology I considered, which is Higher Order Needs I learned to exist for. With my design of the taxing mechanism of this Proposition 63 still viable in our court system and the ballot initiative passing into law, we can see the US President does an obvious take on my direct work and statements in several of my accomplishments over many administrations of the Highest Office in the Land. Take note for those of you in my current and past backgrounds and bring forth examples to me of lifts and thefts you know about.

Woolsey's SMART Security an Improvement
Tue, 2012-10-09 20:08

- Homeland into Foreign Policy

U.S. Representative Lynn Woolsey of California is retiring, and she leaves a legacy of 440 plus speeches on the House Floor speaking about peace and the motivation of taking care of us and helping the American people instead of paying the high cost in blood and money of war. Woolsey stated on 9/11 of 2012 that "helping people costs pennies on the dollar of waging war." She called for SMART Security, which advocates for Development and Diplomacy as the solution to the War on Terror. With Rep. Barbara Lee of Oakland getting the pass on, and with Sonoma-Marin Thoughtfulness and brandishing Service Mark Art like Jann Demystifying Affects(tm), we can land the defense money to build soft skills, educations, and services of people we all are like. Unfortunately with our local history of relationship discrimination in employment and the paving over of natural scenery worth loving, the D and D in discussions can sound like Rape the Land of traditional money interests.

We should shape our foreign policy by our homeland security to include kindness encouragement at the workplace, opportunity nicely at off hours activity, and emotional support bolstered in our homes- all capably administered by freedom offered with money and less restrictive control to make each of all of us right.

Traveling Gives a Grander Feeling for Self
Mon, 2012-09-17 21:01

- Family and Friends

Visiting other places to see people you know is great proof of bonding. Distant relations can count the times each other has seen the other person's house and compare notes on the geographic situation and reunion reasons. The family and friends cementing by traveling as far apart as different states after decades on and off goes a long way to holding forth one's sanity. An individual doesn't have to plan alone; he can rely on more experienced travelers and utilize cost saving accommodations sharing their home as opposed to eating 3 meals out and staying at hotels.

Taking in the geography of the area also helps one's perspective and stability. Seeing more of the world and country add to a person's senses and familiarity that he can see out his eyes and in his "container" as he views his home bound surroundings. This greater freedom once explored can be from sightseeing and pure pleasure socializing, or the feeling is an open responsibility coming from exploring new potential housing and rating services as a by-product of the geographic visitation. People grow developmentally and they grow on you both directions because of in person encounters.

Gain the courage to travel, and you will gain clarity out of an uncertain anxiety and trepidation caused by sameness and stillness. Traveling along with a partner, going to the family or friends' house solo, or meeting up with a relation at a common 3rd port of call can be done when the appropriate consumer's experience and independence can mature in worldliness and acceptable behavior away from the usual.

International Treaty on Medical Punishments
Sat, 2012-08-18 15:30

- Homeland into Foreign Policy

Thinking our doctors and the entire medical and related professions mean "Do No Harm" as the central ethic, do you wonder if other countries and our own corruptions perform human rights abuses with this ethic mistaken? A world class treaty is needed, and Jann Demystifying Affects owning trademarks and copy rights in mental health services and medical counseling shows we're the ones to start this movement. Not punishing through clinical medicine is a needed law in America, is a rampant problem for China because this is seen as a good idea to do, is expected of communist types like Russia as a part of their evilness, and I bet Canada is no worse for stupid things like upstaging the chief medical school graduate.

Behavioral correction of mentally disabled is done legally by asking them to do more chores around the house or natural consequences like their missing the bus without a backup ride. Medical research is needed for human practice, and innocents who do not sign up for military benefits are probably or definitely included without informed consent. Get the informed consent of your patients if the medical center is good. Doctor mistakes that are grossly negligent are malpractice, and yet a lawsuit of this type can redirect your anal digestion from no loyalty except to money class - Who's? Support office staff is also guilty of criminal taking advantage of their customers by fraud, i.e. a person having insurance that is not accepted by that particular doctor office results in higher charges for the patient than one not having any insurance at all.

Jann Demystifying Affects wants to start making a medicine order worth Christ and royalty to form an international treaty approved by the US Senate for medicine to be non-judgmental in doing good wellness and recovery and doing not harm to the patient. This means not condemning and having both enough feeling and intellect to perform, and carrying forth best medicine to people who need the care regardless of patient convictions, attitudes, Americanisms, or eating candy and soda water in the dentist office. Or money to behold is a practical idealism.

Olympics to Get Back to Worldly
Thu, 2012-08-02 11:16

- Motivation

Inspiring athleticism and rooting for the USA is a great source of joy. Taking decades of your life to recover from a psychiatric disability may mean you forgo being in touch with the world. The Olympics on TV and seeing some culture of the world will create a bigger perspective one appreciates. Typical spectator sports in America such as car racing instruct us someone important to you means blocking opportunity when you've been trying for win-win results like the union taught for negotiations.

Getting back to your own self from your student days and finding the Olympics fresh with new sports and a gamut of athletes putting a face to the hard work of being in condition is quite exciting. After watching the Olympics, one can leave the usual, aged body feeling younger and ready for exercise once your motivation is landed on the ground.

Pay Idea Leaders: A More Authentic Economy
Wed, 2012-07-25 10:45

- Property Rights and Ethics

Jobs are real economy in face to face labor, and paying the worker is universally recognized as honest. We need the original source point of the enterprise to be paid economically. My theme of "A More Authentic Economy" means the origin gets paid ownership and economic reward. For our business environment, neither doing a job nor seizing opportunities away from people make capitalism for all its worth. First and/or original concepts and founders need pay for the copies and their own leadership.

Children are affected when we steal the intellectual property from student term papers or big things like the internet. Value Added to an invention can be a major theme mantic element resulting in reaching across the continents. Built from one individual paying the bodily price of emotion or poison and laying out work related to international economic relations home bound. If now an international truth, look to related leadership and verbal ideas and find me in the mix.

Critical Thinking Lives Through Ban
Sat, 2012-07-21 01:31

- Critical Thinking Fighting Suppression

Teachers can say that politicians of the Watergate era blame journalists for President Nixon's resignation. Too much power to people not elected is one lesson taught. The critical thinking model taught from the philosopher Hegel is that of a thesis idea is countered by an antithesis and these two ways or principles are generated into a new synthesis between them. The resulting synthesis then becomes the new thesis for further change by another antithesis when it arrives. Inside the Beltway had to say something during the era. Their words were, "they are all like that."

From then expression was conservative. Newspapers took a dive. Newscasts became less liberal. Media was purchased by Corporate America. The biggest media moguls were from outside the country. Did Power retaliate and hurt people of ideas and imagination and who couldn't write? Has the leadership used medicine to ban ideology and opinions not furthering the objective of "what's in it for me only?"

Who or What Do You Work For?
Mon, 2012-07-02 22:46

- Prevention and Health

A patient with a complicated transaction loaded with emotion for him needs personal support. A grown sibling should be enough, as long as she is not jealous of getting mother's intended shrivel whiter teeth. So then the dentist offices (three of them in total) hardly acknowledge the patient more than a bus line driver. When the final dentist office appears not to have made an appointment when the client checks-in before the scheduled time, the client asks like Five Easy Pieces: "who did you make the appointment for, the money or the patient." It's perfunctory professional to not have customer service principles or have ethics for direct, explanatory relationships. For example, sending email reminders of the appointment to the financially responsible party and not to the patient thereby making unethical reputations like the Medi-Cal eras. I'm sure the one with the purse strings is tight with money, and a reactionary heart is felt true when the financial conservative blames the consumer for his own mental illness. Not liking someone for their teeth can be wrong, and don't blame acne on an intellectual consumer either when opinions are banned in certain offices.

Re: District Elections and the Cookie Cutters
Wed, 2012-06-13 16:34

- Advocacy

As a young boy studying the newspaper I delivered via my bicycle I understood the issues adults had in living in my Santa Rosa. Being called "an issue oriented candidate" by a neighboring state assemblyman during my school board days encouraged my resolve. The social emotional skills of my Teach Peace initiative spirit with critical thinking for history classes is a winner, but when will I get recognized for prior success to bring strength to my justice campaign?

Men of ideas that have merit deserve a seat on the council, and my governance experience as an elected official in education is top of the line. Power Alley and the library crew can re-read my Marquis Who's Who in America bio this September regardless of local politics. If we were to have district elections, it would be natural to select experienced leaders with successful stories from underrepresented communities. Focusing on people we need and not skipping directly to real property values of neighborhoods will bring diversity of constructive opinions that can build our city from the ground up.

Enjoying Nature, Parks, and the Outdoors
Mon, 2012-05-21 11:53

- Reviews and Entertainment

Getting to our basic human nature can be a journey that includes the great outdoors. Taking in the sights and using our physical ability to hike in nature is one key ingredient to finding ourselves. The quiet contemplation of natural beauty with outer prompts of wild animals and birds crossing the way keeps us in tune with our humanity. The wilds are conducive for friends and family to accompany you as well as solitude. A spiritual moment is arrived most each time we act to experience the natural scenery. Enjoying wilderness like our parks is a gift from previous generations and we can always feel grateful for a sanctuary preserved from urban development. Living as a simple being in the present moment evokes awe for utter tranquility that we need to be ourselves. Take part in our natural heritage and visit our parks and enjoy any natural landscape in easy distance to you.

Needs Supported Christian Bible with a Post Script
Sun, 2012-04-29 23:33

- Holistic Community and Perma culture

Our more mass communicative and empathetic societies can acknowledge better the human needs we have outside of basic love and we can keep the word true from Biblical times.

Needs are seen as special trouble to the office, and some parties want the office to run our lives. These same people often use an imprint of far right Christianity and judge the rest inferior. How do clients get work rights when narrow mindedness keeps needs hidden or even bans personal types?

By changing translations of the versions of the Bible to highlight more feelings, we and the future are better prepared to be of empathy. With a modern letter post script after the classic bible passages mostly written by Paul, we can address the needs of people best. Church Elders could write a consistent map of human needs for the Christians themselves and for the religious to be aware of their adversary wherever they may be. We need good people to take care of themselves and prevent harm from those who block or play keep away needs and wants in a standard business motivation model.

Presenting a Christian bible that has an emphasis on feeling language in standard parts and a teaching letter in the modern day on addressing needs, we could propose One Point in a peace plan. Meant for ourselves, youth, prospective converts, Islam in progressive nations, others to understand Christianity does not have to be sacrifice and that the humble can prevent usury and takeus advantageous of themselves. This would be appealing to all those interested in a more practical International Christian ethic well worth a 2nd Protestant Reformation starting in America.

Recommend GIGO for Clean Recovery
Fri, 2012-04-13 10:35

- Prevention and Health

A business data processing course I took for my major at Santa Rosa Junior College formed my basis of my mental health standing. My dream was the international reaching across business with me living comfortably where my heart resided, but the concept I picked up was the computer is only as good as what goes into it. GIGO, or Garbage In Garbage Out was if faulty, extraneous, or redundant data was entered into the system, the results would be in error and correction and redesign was necessary making a delay. I took BDP 52 knowing I was ill with something and I remained thoughtful and full of internalizing for self philosophy in my classes.

My environment was making me lonely, yet my heart of love wanted constant people and family bonds intact for the light when my dark period was traversed best. Keeping myself in a passion and emotional dungeon in regards to other people who I would have liked to be close to felt like an injustice to me throughout these affected decades of my life span. GIGO was lonely because I was at the point of my breakdown and wanted to experience love. My head swam with delusions when my awkward behavior needed a relationship to converse. The de facto GIGO observed in clients arrested in human development and maintaining their tawdry life of substance abuse, etc. is kept by the cultural "salad bowl" of like friends together.

It seems like most people with mentally illness need to change their life around in addictions, jail, and honesty and would best find supports to a healthy lifestyle. I arrived at my mid century a better man with grown family closer than when I was a teenager and with important accomplishments under my belt. My then-part time church employee and student set out for change with my life at my application of the inception of GIGO, and administering my life path has succeeded mostly in affecting the status quo in self and government. There is always more for achievement and in relations like a young at heart person I remain.

Self Made Man
Sat, 2012-03-31 09:09

- Advocacy

A person's unprepared life can be a hard journey. He is self made if the usual supports are lacking in emotions or advice. Commonly we recognize starting out in business, paying for most all a college education, or taking an unknown path from his origins. A family testing the community and giving the son trials can be a testament to sharing, altruistic love, and a giving spirit to see that no one is left out in our culture.

Self made people do not have to be isolated social islands and can have a safety net in place by offers of others and government. A consumer of mental health needs his own participation to recovery. If he keeps his nose clean he can be disabled but free of institutionalization. Striving for health with medicine and care in treatment that is least restrictive can still permit one to be his original basis of a person in his mind's eye. The case for self made can be true when we see others contributing to his life because he sought these supports and earned them. Accept mentoring and guidance to be and reach.

Good Morality is too Rare and to Keep
Mon, 2012-03-12 21:28

- Motivation

Morals and being moral are hard to define. Lawyers say they do not know what morals are. Non-judgmental attitudes about others without your spirit condemning and tolerance to different behavior other than your own are important to carry. Standing strong against moral bankruptcy of your own and putting on a brave face in public after a tarnishing experience known to others calls out for understanding yourself and growth. Belittling gossip, harmful teasing and murderous press about someone's downfall in the first person creates an environment ripe for one's change of heart toward sin. People are unkind to morality. Hypocritical posturing can damage both nice people and the mean spirited. Trying to win life with ethics deeper than business rules is a game often restraining you socially. Morality also gives you good karma if you act known to others. One important tip is the law and courts like a good Christian and advantages can arrive eventually from internal dialog over what is good.

Adding to Someone for Niceness
Tue, 2012-02-21 21:15

- Advocacy

Advocating for rights is legalistic and can be done with attitude. Feelings are not required to have inside of you when the spirit is fighting for what's right. Adding to someone in their life or environmental circumstances like work takes an advocate personally or professionally trying to develop someone. Establishing trusted relationships and kindly coaching to build a person will assist the client learn interdependence like a good friend can do for a person with disabilities. Ignorantly or knowingly permitting a consumer to work on self improvement on his own steps leads to powerful learning. However, appropriate supports are needed to not let a psychiatric disabled person to fend for life wallowing on his own stumbling through life or making big mistakes while suffering. Being appropriate in supporting a person will lead the resurgence in the client's life worth American independence.

"Supervising Target" Credit Specific
Tue, 2012-01-24 20:31

- Property Rights and Ethics

Encouraging IP ownership recovery that was taken from the disabled is worth election and investment. Original source point talent frequently is made poor and hurt in America. Businessmen rarely have a life idea or possess creativity because of the sterile intellect of dollars and sense maximum pressure. Their targets for supplying their profitable ideas are creative people either with behavior out of the norm and are punished for it or the greed takes advantage of human spirits. Aggressive types use a heavy hand both known and unknown to the source at the inception process. If you said it you said it or if you did it you still did it, regardless of disability. The trick then is to get the law to be ethical and come to the side of right ethics in a usually one sided money game. Starts and morals of an idea man once elected in his past can lead the US to a more authentic economy by bridging him, his sanity, and the puzzle of his productive mind. Utilize honor, memory, volume of output, and a legal method suggested to me by a District Attorney employee to make US whole.

Acceptance is Biological Success
Thu, 2012-01-12 12:51

- Motivation

Darwinian Survival of the Fittest is mate selection for reproduction based on individual characteristics applied impersonally. The person's population subset or demographic grouping can determine if the spouse material is socially supported. When we rate somebody one of our own kind and worth talking with, humans begin to duplicate warmth to an individual by accepting someone. The person has met a prima facie element of maintaining and entering the interaction/love stage of Maslow's Hierarchy of Needs.

Using discrimination, castes, and box structured compartmentalization we can isolate people to prevent a basic human need to be matched. These people have fallen through the cracks for whoever's fault, but is it ever too late for their heart to love? What's it worth to fall in love or be yourself to fight the Status Quo made by self interested hardliners to gain what you want and wish for?

Gregg's advice: Employ an individual relationship with God, try hard to result in higher order needs fulfilled based on spirituality, and enhance a practical endeavor like a field of work or study. The owner's example is law and medicine from proactive accomplishment with leadership in mental health and education each. Will this win a spouse and girlfriend, end a war, or advance the space program? It's all three with the Capitols and Hollywood combined when proper credit is given to me as a computer contributor.

Here's to a real lady to recognize Gregg for what he's worth and she brings to him a loving relationship. Gregg Jann Management Science Museum or bust is fun to think about, and credit the author for each of your parts you do if in my name.

Imagination and the Czar of the Pacific
Fri, 2011-12-23 11:57

- Homeland into Foreign Policy

God's gift of fantasy provides escapism and adds to who we are. Ask Playboy magazine and we learn fantasy is the strong part of our sexuality. It is imagination that makes one's way interesting. Creativity bridges fantasy and dreaming to reality by visualizing positive outcomes. Stretching from what is ordinary perception to what is desired with goals and simulations for practice is required beyond our bedroom. Baseball players require visioning by imagining where on the field the ball will go when they step in the batter's box to go to bat. A position like Czar of the Pacific making peace and commerce with prosperity among the Pacific Rim nations starts by thinking up stuff. Living in the present moment is health, and working on CoP in service, business, and spirituality with civilian control is health too. Free speech and changing past practice are processes of an elected official in education who dreams of overseeing an international Navy of protection.

Sub-Human Judgmentalism Discrimination
Thu, 2011-12-01 15:41

- Critical Thinking Fighting Suppression

Judging another person to be sub-human and treating them with discrimination does happen. A court opinion for a word and application to favor economic contract rights to someone law abiding and legally contributory may be necessary for justice in mental health. Being denied rights from public contracts, promotion in paid employment or even just hire rights, and marriage ability calls for legal and financial backing for progressive improvement when an institution rejects someone on traits or attitudes that are not the norm.

Women can choose not like you because of the clothes you are wearing. A form of racism exists generally if sub-human is taken seriously. A person's development and cultural interests can be too rudimentary and low class for a museum curator relationship. If an individual has good morals and works for open minded higher order needs that are accomplished, American society must accept and reward the person with toleration to the other person's law abiding behavior.

Credit: A young Russian woman I met only emailing through online dating suggested the title of this entry which is the only one I have done for others. It is the only request of others I wrote directly although I have a few endorsements in therapy, mental health, and policy and for similar kindnesses from me that affect people the way I intended to with my work and experience. [Thank you wherever you are to recommend myself and Jann DA/Jann Demystifying Affects. I appreciate the nice words and I do hope from good word of mouth. Differences I performed and leading with the ideas expressed were made in the spirit of paid work for vast impacts not just as an Activity Businessman but hoping for profit enough for start-up capital to realize these innovations I set into play. AB is a funny, keep-the-mind sharp tool which is good for civics, social capital, and which is a sleight occupational title for management, those not at paid employment or like the fabled Soccer Moms. Activity Businessmen don't like to hear from people who say AB's are nothing and not worth anything as part of their critic's mean spirited nature and these detractors lack accomplishments basis in their whole outlook on work and life.]

In the past, I was pen pals with maybe 5 Russian females (BDs make more assumed people according to digital photos) that came to me through online dating services. I made quick serial relationships to practice my communication interpersonally because I thought it was safe to write far away with an interpersonal problem. Additionally, I asked one or two of these women that I wanted a Russian Aleksandr Solzhenitsyn Writing Award for critical thinking and producing influences for improvement in standards or in international relations while living and working in Gulag style conditions, mine with a health business license in the latter part of my print journalism career. I may have invented this award at the time of my copy right application, as it doesn't exist without me. I asked my own USA company Finance Advisor for me to be a millionaire from the Russian treasury to be my award to make up for inept bad liability in my social work as counseling employee and chemical prison in personal life. One of these woman wrote to me more of my claims to ownership that I ever wrote women anywhere, in a foreign country or anyone other than intellectual property attorneys. Probably law and censors interfering with (re)production of hidden greatness suppressed.

The author goes back if foreign nations know me like I think it is good for the USA to pay me money, credit, and kindness attention/care directly to show we care about the person Gregg who stated once back from Chico State in 1986, "I think we should protect the inventor at the ballot box." For example, he's a free man with elected honor always with a Governor's Special Message from Hawaii that we can thank Neil. We love the Islands spirit that seems mainly kindness and visualizing to local Sonoma County. The Governor stated Mr. Gregg Jann carried kindness and gratitude to many facets of his work in public service on letterhead. Receiving this commendation is no Act-hole of meanness, albeit in need of friends and wife material. In his figurative mind and brainstorming opinion creativity, I once said the Hawaii thank you word of "mahalo" may mean: kindness all ways except one, for me in person to apologize if pressed. With "kindness all ways except one in person" is my unpleasantness who worked love for others, warmly felt in contentment for greater good accomplishments.

For a gulag example later in Spring 2013, the treatment providers I have did a temporary change in medicine, or it could be from one of 2 lawyers I complained to as I was being a preventive ombudsman. People put into me something without me knowing they broke into my apartment and medicine cabinet for twice saying a swear word and "they" hid a med adjustment for punishment. It gave me Brain Pain to repeat a mistake in a Support Group with an Act-hole not understanding. I was still at writing the project being age regressed ON MY ORDER/REQUEST for creative recovery while suffering and saying the swear words 2 times in my life in slips from his reform dedication.

Other breaking and entering occurred on my federal housing when somebody also 2 times broke into my apartment to steal an art character. It was on a pendant and chain that I either designed in full with describing to a friend of an artist or added a great deal of story to the character from re-memory on a 4th of July in 1979 vacation traveling and camping.... When I was 16 going on 17 years old in Banff National Park I had forgotten I was in a prayer answer in pain and deeply meditative, even perhaps in shock trauma. In British Columbia I wrestled with a bear from playing with his snout while I laid flat on my back on a picnic table bench. After playing with the bear's whiskers and nose and things sharp with my hand while I thought my brother was playing with a branch, I saw her or her cub walking toward me with her nose pointing me to move. I walked away urgently a few steps, immediately at mid step I was slammed to the ground with her soft, heavy paws from behind close by. I used reverse psychology in a recumbent bike mode walking backward flipped face-up and low in his clutches as I cooperated when the bear dragged me some. To prevent being dragged more into the forest, I twisted my body to be in alignment with the front end of the table with my upper body or head held stationary in too dangerous a manner. It worked. The bear shoved me under a picnic table hard like it was his den. I placed both arms in disaster drill mode with one arm protecting my neck below my face and one wrapped overhead trying to protect my neck from behind as much as I could during the incident. My legs were braced against the cement end bottom of the table as he crammed me below, and my upper arm blocked my nose from too much damage as the bear went her seat first to apply pressure to stuff me under there. The bear(s) left me alone as I lay still and barely breathing. When my family of siblings and mother came back they pitched a tent after taking my pulse. In the fall of '79, the injuries made me a high school varsity football bust as I played not enough for a lifelong starter and JV Star back, and caught only 2 passes on the field as a back-up flanker receiver and started some on special teams that kept me proud in let-down. I quit after 3 games on the Montgomery Vikings for feeling angry, I thought for not playing as much as I hoped to and planned. Now I wonder if Santa Rosa City Notice from my police report in Spring 2013 on the stolen jewelry piece or something else me is our current good luck in opening talks with Iran and Russia. News on TV said the US is finally gaining international cooperation worth trust to the US leadership over chemical weapons. The prayer answer was hoping that summer before the Iran Hostage Crisis that I would create the US Peace Department in my future career, which I have worked at in my management information systems degree, counseling career and post life more than my centerpiece/figurehead. July of 1979 was near the signing into law with President Carter and the full US Congress passing the Education Department into federal cabinet level.

On the Gulag theme, I was punished as a consumer of talking and listening to peers who are patients. We're hurt and offended by how rough it is to be ignored in human comeuppance which is why I said it somewhat delusional in anger as I didn't feel being returned love in any way except for mother. The only other swearing of slurring more than one label spoken in my lifetime was in my lawyer's office. At my first visit I was dramatic in looking for my lucky break for many intellectual property things looking for lots of money in the year of forming my sole proprietorship. I used poetic license intentionally for impact to invent or at least call attention to a need we could fulfill if we took a chance for change in history for a black man president that I have hoped much in my life. We won. I was thinking presidential rivals are mistreated for prognostication of many terms or simply designing one candidate when a whole team does most all. I intended no harm for this rare story of scatology and am sorry if I offend anyone. I was target of one of my cussing in asking for social favor of being an isolated trucker for 75 hour weeks while keeping part time employment at the same time as counselor several nights and weekends. Gregg_at_N.O.W gets a bad definition for reforms and advocacy for encouragement, and those two slanderous words did me a bad reputation places if goodness is not taken seriously in morals.

To crack my skull internally to remember pre-5 years old and other great legendary things I'm working on before setting out for this writing project is an uncomfortable process that I asked for and medical staff agreed to do it because of long suffering. My original family has been thoughtful in civil rights as our father the minister traveled to Mississippi in the 60s and we have home videos of him marching on a court house in the South. I am strong in keeping his early spirit and my impression of the USA 1960s is To Protest like protestant faiths of Christianity. My application of my working heart as an adult is mostly for people with psychiatric disabilities with other populations included in my verbal officiating. My resume is service economy as a win/win union negotiator not long ago in Century 2000s, now a sole proprietor. An influence parallel is my National Minister father inviting Ceasar Chavez to the 1st Presbyterian Church in Santa Rosa when Mr. Chavez was fighting for field worker rights in the 60s or 70s.

The Defense Mechanism
Wed, 2011-11-16 19:00

- Homeland into Foreign Policy

Perhaps setting the government precedent for the principle of this blog category, Reagan hired Weinberger twice. The man in question was called Cap the Knife and cut the California Health and Human Services Department under Governor Reagan. Then President Reagan hired Cap No Limit to head Secretary of Defense for no limit on spending. This was done with no heart for love. Can we even talk about it after all these years?

Defense is too heavy handed for the intolerant rules and case interpretations that create police state roles in the minds of social service clerks. Unemotional Security harms people by being inhuman to needy people who need help processing. Using kindness and a gentler policy bringing to state agencies more ability to support people is the first step. Providing a care comparison to foreign nations that benefits both nations' populations is more like it.

Warning after 11/11/11: I got acne whiteheads on my forehead and lost a tooth at the dentist office both this month as meds were forcibly changed in a trial, a Japanese beer was consumed, and the church met a visitor while I was working there. It's a knighthood type story with jousting I did not volunteer for that befell the above criticism around Veterans Day of my first communication to the White House (see Chapter 2). Learning to smile with a professional care to undo a medicine drugging to have no personality since psychiatric treatment began in efforts from beautiful female nude dentistry prior to this month while I was trying to be monogamous with some phantom woman on one hand and still untried virginity on awareness on the other is completely unpredictable in behavior. I gave a kick with swearing later in the chair of a later, different dentist at the above entry's time while I was reporting this uncertain nude contact at least twice because I'm a nice man. This month my then-dentist gave me a shot in my gum at the site of my college broken jaw, received when I was playing middle linebacker on intramural flag football. Radical behavior to and from, big as The White House or small as a tooth; can cause consternation and suspicion on decay things we don't see.

Way back in the 1980s I criticized Cap/Reagan in a CSU, Chico business class for using needs against people/workers and telling managers to use people's needs more whether this is backhand or true. I had talked to a Butte County attorney in private practice to ensure growth of computer classes and my option as a Management Science major would remain available to me in legal utilization of strategies I expected to be controversial. It is learned helplessness if I were to think talking to the lawyer did THINGS, because as my late father told me in his retirement: "Lawyers will do nothing to you." I do not know if I was punished in the work places because of talking to a lawyer or writing print journalism or remaining single morality. Did nothing favor of lawyer hurt the making of the WWW in California and other pluses in our economies, opposite Jesus Christ and his teachings? My work for origin, design, peace, and more than one chances morality advocacy are great economy and are Christian liberal. My great experience is as a recognized public official with a track record; I have seen a lot of hurt while working middle or line in many collars represented occupationally for several experiences I share and improve on like the counselor and consultant I am and as candidate for higher office if ever needed.

The conservative capitalism of self worth is, "Not you at all, and I only mean money in all I do." There's a strong theme of screw you in all elements belief, budget and butting heads to get along interactively. Big Money says in its lack of heart to men seeking victory for the social/economy of the nation and world, "no quarter" and does not give in to anyone. Even their institutions of creative credit and economy and organizational structures repel and suppress an innovative man leading kindness.

Does it hurt to ignore the author, and do we make strong if we lead to his gain and health and his own family? The innocent author has seen good news and bad news in macro at times of extraordinary instances of his own achievements recognized, and unrecorded in revolutions and economic lead indicators. Is this man American royal of greater effects? Russia hates royalty, and he read personally and indirectly to that affect. A Japanese candidate for state office as a San Francisco State University management employee bestowed The Honorable Gregg Jann. He endorsed her as a Sonoma Democratic Central Committee member, worth milking. In an in-house job interview for a former employer for vocational services in Marin, a Far East woman recognized first ever stating to him, "You are self proclaimed royalty." Rightful credit for any creator authentic may need new laws or just the attention of these angles to improve economy and the money and the world's foreign affairs. It is wrong to say author doesn't deserve wealth and presidential health care. His Mr. means no harm to/from all we are and we should have "help/let me up" better in his no time for his own hoped for wife. He has his own meaning to his bestowed title, whether agreed to by Carole H, that we should realize and which is theme of writing Book II.

Gratitude, Saying Thank You With Feeling
Sat, 2011-11-05 07:24

- Holistic Community and Perma culture

A deeper sense of being grateful for what you have is important for a true meaning from our country. In today's world each person who gives thanks for the vast wealth we in the USA are known for helps produce more justice for the understanding displayed. Deserve the feelings that make a human modest. Being grateful creates a humbleness from spiritual centering meaning each of us relies on other people and a supernatural peace. Self made traits are a pride, however notice gifts we can provide and those that were given to us. Acknowledge the bounty in material, emotions, or spiritual; whether survival level or prodigious, with an authentic clarity.

To prosper with abundance in spirit, be grateful for all you have and that which you can give.

Show up in person and say aloud "thank you" to people doing you nice by good deeds or in words to you. Politeness gets along on the surface and if not manipulative can open the door to more emotional depth. Appreciating kindness is wholesome and vital for good karma. Notice the good stuff in your life with meditation, prayer, words, and actions meant for the source to know you appreciate the loving kindness.

Psycho-Social Rehab to Internalize Behavior
Wed, 2011-10-19 21:58

- Critical Thinking Fighting Suppression

Suppression comes from a structure or hierarchy that forces a restriction on a person's liberty. Suppression can have positive affects as in decreasing appetite with herbal supplements that are healthy and effectively lose weight. Suppressing a person's psychiatric symptoms by behavioral correction can feel irritating at the point of intervention, but in the long run rehabbing and modifying is most conducive to appropriate behavior once internalized. Five positive statements to every negative comment is the guideline for behavior modification. Behavior Mod is not enough for disability recovery. When psychiatry, medications, room and board, and daily program activities are present and all contingent on change and transforming adult independence in the community, psychosocial rehabilitation is the discipline utilized. Attitude and motivation then become the keys for someone improving one's life once emotional stability, access and money is set for a good length of time.

Public Administration Needs Me
Fri, 2011-09-30 12:56

- Property Rights and Ethics

Being educated and trained with a university degree as a systems analyst, I went to job interviews at Chico and in Sonoma stating my immediate goal was to be an end-user systems analyst. The employers I applied to denied me. Perhaps the validity of the design of their management information systems for workers with a computer caused tangential fear of the term meant customers or elements not for bosses. Did they fear the direction of efficiency would not result in more money for the organization?

It was wrong on their part and somewhat podunct to not favor my business administration degree and ideology production with published commentaries while in more than 2 colleges in general employment for management. If some people see you're good then do they want you hurt in a tit for tat manner.

For an agency like Social Security, class warfare is not an issue when system change can be revenue neutral in designing user friendly policy and procedures. Consumers, top executives, retirees, providers, line staff, government bureaucrats all need access to computers directly and indirectly. Ownership of idea generation to the source point and rewarding idea people sounds revolutionary to usury, stealing, asshole denizens and decision makers. Stating "I hope your heart is not set on" end user systems analyst is adversarial management not fully understood without experience in career paths and applications of an individual's own philosophy.

Those employees with principles and practices have parted organizations with philosophical differences. This is the central mind and initiator of reform and progression as a spur change agent to paramilitary structures in medicine for the mind. The mental health system rates an applicant for work and contract low for being a victim of violence at a prior contractor, and they need the same elected official's plan for their current revenue. Take another day off to think about it.

Blocking goodness people with the money and top-down style preferring status quo, substance abuse, and forensics is not a quality region. Force used on morality to be like kind or destitute through discrimination and social dungeons caused disability and harmed this nation.

Recognize people who contribute more than taxes to their country. We don't in Town Known for Bad P*****. See my elected career on a school board and private company building reform through the ballot box as examples. We need Sonoma County Legal and Medical professions to recognize the accomplishments both I am and those used economically dating back to college to make a more authentic economy with rightful ownership and rewards both tangible and intangible.

Wishing a Person Well in Deeds and Words
Thu, 2011-09-15 18:03

- <u>Family and Friends</u>

Prayerfully sending good thoughts to significant people, even adversaries and torn romances, helps stabilize feelings of good karma. Words spoken of good luck and a sound future for the other are important to the receiver and keep up spiritual connectedness. Yet regret I have is the remorse felt in a phantom lover relationship when I felt grateful and wanted goodness for her, yet the words she requested of "wish me well" seemed like it should go without saying. I had to say it when she was saying goodbye, but I had an attitude. Even if feeling disrespected and hurt on my side, she knows she needs relief from guilt and shame in her treatment of me.

Love inside of us needs expression. Disabled people don't realize their kindness is not always appreciated. A consumer of mental health is most likely overlooked in straight-ahead competitive relationships. A naturally unfriendly or at least unpleasant demeanor, a rough (il)legal existence, or simply expensive dynamics at work and on the tax rolls all add up to a lack of acceptance from normal people to someone offering love. The end game of love peace needs deeds and words that the best is our wish for them in active intentional living.

How Real Planet of the Apes Movies?
Wed, 2011-08-17 20:26

- <u>Reviews and Entertainment</u>

Viewing the <u>Rise of the Planet of the Apes</u> was an intellectual delight of topical issues and a throwback to my childhood. Seeing what seems like 5 or so movies of this brand as a youth were a fascinating and exciting critique of the brutality of mankind shown most entertainingly. The current prequel film now showing looks kindly to human parents and the need for medicine research for aging seniors. All too many mental health consumers can be likened to being used for medicine research by a profession that doesn't know how its medicines work. The value of the portrayed medicine to my movie sidekick who is my mother is as real to me as what I get prescribed for me. Gaining greater stability and increasing range of emotion to go along with enhanced intelligence that I feel psychiatry medicines can do for the disabled is worth animal experimentation to this environmentalist.

As an elected official in education I'd advocate the character education advantages of a good boy-and-"his"-mountain lion story as an empathic tear jerker as a guess suggestion for the classroom. This Apes movie is better for pointing out empathy for the splitting point of a parent who couldn't protect his young as honestly as the ape Caeser enjoyed freedom with his own kind. That scene shed my emotions.

As far as my San Francisco experience goes as a Woolworth Assistant manager, we would have rooted for the apes if one of them talked. The animal keeper was an ass. The public safety crew was just doing its job that it had to do. The police shooting the side of a bus which was toppled in a rampage in the movie was reminiscent of the actual Supervisor Milk riots, which by happening at night was pretty terrifying to those teenagers of us up North of the Bridge back then. The modern day movie was Just a fantastic science fiction tale that felt fact-based and greatly human.

Moves Up for Independence
Fri, 2011-08-12 22:58

- Property Rights and Ethics

Shifting one's place of residence for less than gargantuan changes does not always make a difference in a person's life. Think about your own problems and weigh-in at the source to determine if making a change would be a fitting solution. Find the support you have in friends, family, and social agencies and take a leap if your support system does not go away when the benefits of the new housing situation add to your life. Think wisely about financial arrangements and pay heed to the security of your income, if necessary the family contribution, and government entitlements if qualified.

Genuine luck can be obtained in right living. Stages in Maslow's Hierarchy of Needs and the Stages of Being are two models worth consulting in our development because multiple housing arrangements over time can raise a person's awareness and perspective. A series of moves will highlight experience in a person's American life. The right situations that are timely for immediate needs or for the long haul can dramatically change a person living alone or with casual roommates. Even bad living modes can have payback.

Having roommates is a good common experience to live through part of your life. Family as an adult single can be a stable influence. Living alone later can be a Godsend. Coupling up in relationship and marriage is not always a goal, yet in the psychology field living together makes a qualification for professional jobs and management dependencies. Think Win-Win in your moving to increase your station in the world you live.

Love Month is July or August
Sat, 2011-07-16 14:42

- Advocacy

Assessing an individual to have a lack of empathy seems very wrong. Professionals in their offices intentionally make themselves inhuman over their "true" care judgment. Psychiatry condemns clients without helping their patients in their own rude attitude of their work life. Charges that one doesn't love in concern and compassion can be rightful for the public in civil discourse about the Speaker of the House as ABC's The View put it on the air in November of 2010.

Is he a lead and product of Republicanism who looks down on Americans who do not possess success, luck, or family? In a sports analogy of both relate-ability and ability, I think of a star baseball Oriole who once later managed the SF Giants. He did not succeed as the manager because he didn't understand players with more ordinary talent and make them a winning team that year.

Inability to relate to others is often a normal wall and a chasm, but it is wrong to say out loud someone is devoid of human spirit in feelings. It is required kindness to know mankind best seek to have concern to needs of people. Anything else calls out for a name for the condition and for it to be rehabilitated out of existence wherever in society it is. How can anyone surmise such be an inhuman for his development without understanding a chosen bible and the specific needs of the target directing goodness to man?

Untainted Experience Saved from Spoiling
Sat, 2011-07-09 13:54

- Motivation

In a strategy that lasts a lifetime, mostly save the best available experiences for later. Try your best to keep in contact with family, relatives, and close relations. But like owning the best car you will ever have at 19 years old, using up the best things in life now will spoil anyone down the road. Keeping experiences in check saves marriages. Fresh and exciting works like a rocket to consumers rebounding in a big way from a life of ill feelings.

The freshness principle works on all surprises. By delaying some good vacation places, not going to the trendy restaurant hole-in-the-walls immediately, or not knowing the best hidden features right nearby until stumbled upon more well helps spur rejuvenation. Waiting until one is not depressed, confused, or sleepy is a gamble that pays off later for clients with serious mental illness. When one is more recovered, he can fully appreciate freshness and enjoy those experiences more because he did not taint his views with bad feelings that he felt earlier in his life. This strategy is a gamble that one will recover and those experiences need to be sure things that will be there for him for this to work.

Keeping in Touch
Fri, 2011-06-24 16:12

- <u>Family and Friends</u>

Family reunions are a mixed bag. The older generations generally love the reconnecting with siblings, aunts and uncles, and children. These things take great organizing and a lot of work, and usually women lead the way. Family reunions can be large or small, and can be rare in your family or more of a regular thing. To be included in plans, the key is to keep in touch with siblings as you grow older.

Keep informing your original family of your whereabouts and your activities, as well as any special relative to you. Phone calls, emails, letters, and cards are connecting rods of a long distance family. An annual Christmas card with notes summarizing the year you yourself are having may keep them aware of you. Mailing cards with personalization on their birthday is a nice commemoration for anyone receiving a Birthday card.

Invest in Talented Names
Thu, 2011-06-02 08:55

- <u>Property Rights and Ethics</u>

Sonoma County, California's blacklisting of Gregg Jann, a local man of significance, tax innovation, and perseverance, is a stench spewing on history. Washington, D.C. succeeds more when the owner of Jann Da and the author of this blog is recognized. Managers need a correction, and it will boost kindness to understand a civic leader doing business.

A-Hole Management school ideology seems prevalent, at least in So Co dating back to New York Giants baseball over 1/2 a century ago. Hiring only those people who you like is unfair, harms diversity, and discourages innovation. Being tolerant to ideas and people and accepting the workers making the good contributions is the best business practice.

All individuals need emotional support, and the ability to enjoy the day. The general discrimination of "whomever I like" that currently is preferred by management makes for un-Christian partiality as warned in the bible (James 2:1). People-oriented progress and supporting lifestyles ostensibly make a good environment, but only if inclusive. An area known for nearby marijuana, wine, and a smoking section high school in my time is not conducive for friendship for the owner's strict morals. Ethics and influence is right money.

Regression Analysis for Recovery
Wed, 2011-05-18 17:44

- Critical Thinking Fighting Suppression

Statistical modeling studied long ago in college molded my experience by thinking regression analysis. This method analyzed dependent and independent variables along the X and Y axis, with a line of best fit. The line can be seen as experience with the data formulated to estimate probabilities for forecasting. Whether or not if used in professional medication studies, these courses assisted me in applying my life path with appropriate correction and interventions keeping me true to myself hood. With a low test of mean squares, the journey taken can be realized as an accurate projection from the starting origin. We can imagine a life can be authentic to himself even with a bevy of psychiatrists, therapists, and miscellaneous supports when one is alert throughout his path taken on the road day or night. Thanks Chico State, and if only a professor or student send Jann Demystifying Affects a modeling study in mental health for win/win enhancement and innovation.

Egg Whites Only to Control Cholesterol
Fri, 2011-04-29 13:41

- Prevention and Health

Eat egg whites to control cholesterol which is a sentenced factor to you from age or medication. Weight gain is a side effect of psychotropic medications. Mental health professionals may deny this. Either they are blind to their treatment M.O., or they supra are using strategy on when to tell us. When fighting fires, feelings and psychosis are more immediate concerns of most disabled people than the long term effects of obesity conditions. Healthy diet selections, portion control, and exercise will help contain elevated cholesterol as one risk factor, along with more medication. The rule is to avoid or reduce consumption of eggs, whole dairy, and red meat. Choose egg whites and if not available eat chicken, fish, or something vegetarian when eating in or dining out. Egg dishes are often paired with unhealthy high cholesterol foods like cheese, sausage, or bacon. Sticking to (yellow dyed) egg whites will keep a tight wire on what to eat by helping a person's resolve.

Community Rehab for Productive Kindness
Sat, 2011-04-09 13:08

- Holistic Community and Perma culture

Criminalizing the strange harms our social fabric. Reporting to someone on the behavior of a third party, it could be anyone loved or not, instead of talking directly to your target with guidance leads to forgotten people and a cold place for you. This informing without educating, counseling, or coaching in a kind form to correct creates no understanding. In other words, snitching instead of caring is wrong, unless there is gunfire in your ghetto. Rehab people so they grow inside of them and you will gain experience and appreciation respect. Law enforcement types like employment lackeys inappropriately administer justice when a person (or non-human in psychiatrist mindsets) has never been engaged in a connection that mentors, guides, teaches, and directs civil warmth that's personal. Observers who try to honestly get others in trouble without enough regard to a solution for earning the greatest humanity are doing less than one dedicated to the greater good.

Passing the buck in not providing feedback and input to a person, coworker, or peer before complaining to civic authorities or supervisors may generate hearing costs at your goal. You did not favor your country by withholding support of a stronger nation by ignoring in person people who may be needy at first. Your intolerant anti-cohesive shortcuts harm community building. They need to develop, you need to try to communicate directly, and both sides of this game need to include each other for maturity.

Peer Counseling Adds Intelligence
Tue, 2011-03-29 14:10

- Property Rights and Ethics

Owning yourself in feelings, thoughts, and intelligences requires boundaries. Extending reach by stepping through boundaries makes for spice in life, creativity struggling, and it can be leadership attributes that appear like needy time wasting to the status quo. Crossing boundaries is almost illegal in psychology jobs, but how else would consumers have the opportunity for employment? By contributing to others, saying what you've learned, and conveying insights using your judgment one can be greatly beneficial to a peer. Your listener will gain perspective, perhaps admire your outlook, and will gain in respect for self and others. It's worth a professional peer counseling pedigree if your valor is open and the sharing you do on the job gains wisdom for your clients.

Glorious Moment by liberal Mainline
Mon, 2011-03-07 19:44

- Holistic Community and Perma culture

Since the last part of the 20th Century an issue with the Church has been its relevancy to our times. I found an increased understanding of people when the church I attend acknowledged recovery. Disability, addiction, and illness oftentimes are called un-American, but the conditions are not illegal in and of themselves. Lying, cheating, and getting oneself in jail are not positive effects, but innocence is one method to good care and love from respect you need. This past Sunday I read Psalms 51 before my congregation, and in the process I found I didn't like the versions that seemed to emphasize sin. I take the passage to be about peer counseling, as teaching "rebels" as one of them from a compromised situation. Beware of the "burnt offering" of being abused by the system, etc. in your providing an example and bringing forth care. Its best liberal Main line Protestant churches to understand and accept people in recovery, and its wise for the consumers to not manipulate and to prevent usury of the religious people.

Building Qualities with Financials
Fri, 2011-02-18 14:02

- Property Rights and Ethics

Trust and faith are important qualities to develop inward of the self and in others eyes. Financial property like taxes requires person backup and known agreements regarding standing of rep payees and conservators. When one is a mental health consumer, the life is difficult for others to accept you with bearing in trust, integrity, and property. Paid work helps, but people being confident in you is more than a job. Being ladies and gentleman on honesty, vices, and discretion sustains generally, in recovery or not. Improving a consumer's image takes reaching across as equals sharing with appropriate peers, family, and those who know you and laying it on the line to gain respect. Try for advisory support if crossing financial boundaries like obligations review risks the person whom you made yourself into.

Love Indirect Now Needs Person Payback
Fri, 2011-01-28 17:13

- Family and Friends

To love someone in return can take an indirect love movement. Know love from someone bigger than you see of him. I added tools from an elected position in education hoping for a Nobel Peace Prize 25 years late now if properly recognized. Bring a good person or virgin to him in the form of a beautiful woman if he has only gotten unrequited love in his lifetime to compensate for holy justice.

Aside from the usual criteria of presidential advisor or promiscuity wisdom, an expressed heart can be priceless to most all if accomplishments gained are contributory to the greater good and/or your own mission.

This ideology can be exemplified by writing and speaking on a school district's goal and success indicator document. It can be shown in negotiating for consumer labor rights in a labor contract. And it can add up from advocating for Generation Y principles in ecology and spirituality as a youth, then taking Gen Y to quotes from a management motivation theory before Gen Y and Gen X were chaptered in the media.

"You ran the most Christ-Like government" is a weird statement taken in modest stride by me as a compliment from a sane superintendent. To return a love good to you and probably your community as it should be is what is ethical.

Step in with people worth inner and outer beauty, both of style and substance, if changing to peace and love is unpleasant within him and others in the dutiful battles and argumentations for the era.

Return to the Big Lover of Indirection with what you as his receiver relates to as important to humans to the giver in person; for dignity, respect, care, health, and love. Understand if he skipped his ages in generational friends as he is moral and young at heart in casting away debauchery and suspect kindness engagement.

Write Gregg Jann at the information on this web site's Contact Us page or be in person at the usual places in San Francisco and Sonoma County. Gregg is the only one seeing the information from his contact info. Wish me a Happy Valentine's Day with praises, invitations, and riddance of impedances. In turn I wish you and yours similar goodness in making holidays worth their meanings.

Bolstering Our Weaknesses
Thu, 2011-01-06 04:27

- Homeland into Foreign Policy

It's vital for our national focus in dealing with other nations to compare the underrepresented populations and make best people of our own country. The economy, nuclear disarmament, global warming and women's rights appear to be the top foreign policy agendas next to settling the current warfare in the Middle East. As soon as we can, we need to change the course of history and lead into a viewpoint of the biblical Book of Mathew's "taking the care of the least of these." With business and practical matters leading global interaction, religion and human love need to strive for social and economic justice, which means more safety and security for the underprivileged. Improving living conditions affects the poor and powerless more than can the wealthy move in their heart. Not merely shallow pride, but an abundance of spiritual wealth can be obtained in making each individual and family healthy and comfortable from the means of nations. Peace will transcend on earth if we advocate and work for strengthening our weakest socioeconomic populations and collaborate on the most vexing problems of the common.

New Year's Resolution: Goodness
Fri, 2010-12-24 18:15

- Motivation

Stand for Goodness for others. Include yourself but don't count your own suffering as deserving to me in and of itself. Add EBU (Emotional Banking Units) strategically and profusely wherever you are to invest in kindness deeds. Being nice to people in person, supporting causes and charities, and furthering progressive movements will not cause you to finish last. These types of generosity of spirit will keep you motivated, build spiritual strength and lead happiness steps for yourself. Don't manipulate support and don't think foremost what kindness will generate for you for a truer priority on the top of your mind. Create a greater understanding within you for others while enhancing more inclusiveness for individuals and for the nation.

Exercise of a Life Worth a Medal
Thu, 2010-12-02 01:13

- Advocacy

The Transformer can be a medal given to individuals worth distinction, courage, sworn oaths of loyalty and protection, and an enlightened spirit of achievement. I've quickly spotted the shape of a Christmas tree on my blog page with writing inside, and this paragraph is a response in my mind. Someone positively impacting the lives of others through accomplishments is not easy. Changing ways of life for Americans using Big Hearted Valor, whether known or unrecognized, can be more significant while soldiers are in combat overseas. Improving living conditions here in America and hopefully changing oneself for the better can be quite a successful undertaking for people from elected officials in education to high minded idealists in recovery from a disability. Drawing out a paper Xmas Tree and making art with branches of your influences, presents of feelings from the abundance of spirit underneath, and the star of Hope stating what guided you through the process for the past can make meaningful presentations for peers, staff, and families.

Administrative Law for the Individuals Served
Fri, 2010-11-12 02:05

- Advocacy

With control of both houses of Congress split between the two major parties, the next star to come along is with administrative law. The policy, regulations, and rules of bodies like Social Security, Medicare, Medicaid, and even state and privately run agencies can either be obstructionist or streamlined.

The best ideas make less run around on the leg work for clients and punish less through principle. The missions of the respective agencies need core beliefs of kindness with the direction of efficiency aimed from the recipients of the service. Even private organizations like non-profits, HMOs and the employment world's human resources departments need the legalese to be working for its clients and customers. The minutiae and attitudes of the bureaucrats call for the focus to be on the citizens of need. The rate payer charges are not the dialogue. Don't hinder consumers as usual and always know who the work is for in the first place, which is the safety net that are supports meant for whoever needs them at emergency or can't do.

World Series is National Play
Sun, 2010-10-24 23:38

- Reviews and Entertainment

Professionals in mental health will say to their clients that watching news is not beneficial to recovery. Newscasts can be alarmist and portray extremes. Dwelling on bad news all the time will not comfort the anxiety-plagued person. Sensory, physical, and emotional experience through recreational activities is salve to the soul. Sports fans of their teams can think of the people who they enjoyed talking with or going to the stadium, reminding them of family and places, and the teams and regions represented that are favorites can warm the heart now from the past and present. The Phoenix major metropolitan newspaper reporting San Francisco's winning the National League Pennant with a page 8 story in the sports section the following day signals something when Texas is front page sports with a picture and big headline the day before. Conservative politics ignore champions from an area that is more respectful of diversity seems to be the culprit to me. The college crowd gets it more with the Cal Bears blowing out of ASU garnering football coverage in circles of people who live and believe in one way thinking . Without the dastardly dislike of someone for the team they root for, think of the best pitching in major league baseball boding well for the San Francisco Giants in post season games.

Extra Legal, Extra Special and Harm
Sun, 2010-10-03 17:04

- Critical Thinking Fighting Suppression

The San Francisco 49ers losing games by making a lot of mistakes appear exciting in highlights to disinterested women. Is the coach playing more unmarried men that attract women than expected at season's start? A study on turnovers in the NFL and relationship status could/has affected business if ever measured. With the county employer preferring significant others in hiring, I question the ability and legality of managers and those of liking. Being extra legal, extra special as intended standing and not through over caution appears illegal to dislike except where harm is an intended product and result as part of the package. What's more right and ethical to mental health system and federal health centers? Employers like extra and do harm to you if they do extra for you. We in the US need to extend my Integrity Recovery Ideas with Gregg Jann in control of the inception, process, and rewards to correct the people and leaders of an economy not yet ethical.

Art Appreciation Helps Talking
Fri, 2010-09-17 00:17

- Reviews and Entertainment

Creative expression can be artistic, beautiful, and peaceful to the mind. The arts can be a meditative practice drawing and releasing breaths of life for the artist. To enjoy a work of art as an object, a person can look for intrinsic attributes of a piece that appeals to his inner person through senses and feelings. "Talking about art or talking about the making of art" is a great concept to encourage insight and conversation skills. Contemplation about history, considering changes of movements and their acceptance by society, or admiring what one can't do as good in artistic ability is all fun to share verbally with someone at least as much as those solo escapes into museums. If you want to be a doer, look for arts classes to express the person you are and find art showings on display and participate by attending.

Medical Consequences Call Out to Be Positive
Tue, 2010-08-31 17:07

- Prevention and Health

"For whom is treatment for" raises questions that the patient may be 2nd, 3rd or 4th in priority. When community members affect doctors and the treatments decided upon are based on punishment of emotions and attitudes, then the client must advocate with the ombudsman until the medical consequence is mitigated. Persons with disabilities are called dead people by many in society. I can't wait to see Get Low when it plays locally at the theater, which is a film about a hermit asking for storytelling at his own funeral party while he is alive. Writers, inventors, and all creative eccentrics appreciate unknown influences being made known. The ordinary psychiatric disabled are denied hearing their story. Others greed, jealousy, and plain spite can block consumers, even if they are not accomplished members of Who's Who. A good rule to the doctor is positive, honest communication and I think also trying to be contributing members of society is important to quality of care. These go along with insight to your own condition as important to quality care. The objectives of working for the President of the USA, the family, or the "hermit" with the illness is not as straight-forward to the medical profession as they need to be.

Consumer Marriage - Love Asexually the Masses First
Sun, 2010-08-15 16:40

- <u>Family and Friends</u>

Being open and affirming is taken religiously to offer someone related-ness, acknowledgment, and encouragement through kindness and spirituality. Consumers and most all people with disabilities have self centered traits in a range of constriction. Being tolerant and non-judgmental to others who may seem strange to your upbringing is necessary. Understanding different types of people will improve consumers' gentleness. Concern and to get along will develop ability to survive on a baseline in the fringes of life. Adding care to your life is best by spreading love to many asexually. This way a person proves he carries love before he picks one out to give and receive his best love. By doing public good and giving of oneself directly to persons he gains a heart worth loving by a rare find and she chooses to join him in his journey of life. May religion and justices recognize marriage is to be love for each other after successful processing of enculturation, adult independence, and mature emotional love which appropriate to each of both of 2 spouses to be.

Add: The above entry was referred to in my Marquis Who's Who pseudonym of Presidents' "August Tip" when meeting with a Private Eye who had international connections. I signed a contract and turned over my last $700 dollars of SDI in December of 2010 in a contract hold to locate money for my role and bone fide contributions in originating, planning, and design of Prop 63 in California of Fall 2004 while meeting with state lobbyists and department workers and management. I was looking for a potential legal case and information to gain money for designing tax legislation that passed popularly or with war powers that transformed the California mental health system for the meeting. My entrepreneurship is based in mental health for work published here and for my Customer Service/Hold economy with its kinder, gentler nation of people over the "screw you" of seize the day capitalism at every turn, which means nothing to you ever at all in the economy of people relating.

The meeting continued when the PI said it was good for business and I described hits in the Middle East rarely visiting my blog. I informed her I didn't know if the FBI's Most Wanted was still alive, and told her passionately to look for him with her Ambassador credentials to locate him using "August Tip" for a work group or to do anonymous field work. The pseudonym is a play on using names of family on my late father's side. A.T. shares words of advocacy in the above month for several years, mainly as one demographic member and helping another demographic group I am not to try to develop a strategic alliance for work and a filled Civil Rights hole is who Americans are.

The PI then pulled out a plastic device in the flower arrangement and said the meeting was bugged. We exited quickly and I told her outside from a distance to cash the check. I didn't get much further on the MHSA funds from this business connection who I met through the Sonoma County Bar Association, but some months later received a phone call with an accent that stated the caller was "president of" and I reeled into her peace motivation to capture or kill the terrorist. Egyptians moved downstairs soon after, and I never knew where the phone call was from except heard I was on a radio station a couple of years later from an unreliable treatment provider. My NOW application is dated accurately herein for an innocent "coincidental evolutionary" in somebody stealing me and my plans where elsewhere wants them.

It is a joke to call that terrorist the national friend for his taking space and an important role in our lives through tragedy. It is wrong to even consider him my business partner even though I heard of reward not yet given to me.

My peace filled role of productivity and creating district attorney justice out of a reform need in the legal community as well as mental health goes well with my religious ambition in Protestant Churches for a living Christianity more inclusive. A nice entity like me works for what I can think of the 3 spellings of profit for money, prophet for greater understanding which means love in more ways like Religion is supposed to, and "proffett" for win/win in feelings on earth like small emotional transgressions are forgiven as we try to make each other feel well together or when alone.

I wanted this above blog entry to make the California Supreme Court as they were deciding Gay Marriage, which bores me in a Reconciling Congregation at church advocacy. I want strategic alliances to gain personal wedding ability and get an actual straight wife who's beautiful, as well as strategic alliances to make international headway on the problems vexing the common like weapons of mass destruction. I have a bear story too, that goes well when I want to pull it out for my legend that I pray for international solution and there are other personal stories in my lead examples. The Man, The Myth, and The Legend is what I called myself at age 20 in Whitney Hall dorm men's room, and I have continued the marquee without much bravado or even outward conversation of someone living in hiding from too much accomplishment from a Process Economy.

Consumers and Diversity Part I
Sat, 2010-07-24 20:21

- Critical Thinking Fighting Suppression

Upward social mobility, quoting Bettering the World in an article I wrote in college, is a sacred belief that Americans must act for and protect. With respects to locally made workers and community members, including diversity of geography, different colleges, and utilizing affirmative action type programs bring some interest to work. Opportunity can expand fairness horizons worth any stripe of civil rights. Individuals should bring their varied experiences and new perspectives for additional ideas and local excitement. One's hard won past assists American innovation if diversity is applied well and excellently to all concerned individuals. Mental Health consumers are worth civil rights movements, not only out of forced poverty. Massive discrimination from people on the streets to employment and housing affects consumers. Seen as consumers' champion, government discriminates by denying social mobility to talent that is both legal and which is needed by society.

Detroit and Morals - an Emerging Movie Genre
Wed, 2010-07-14 02:23

• <u>Reviews and Entertainment</u>

The latest art house commercial movie playing locally titled <u>The Solitary Man</u> portrays moral themes understandably and complex enough by including women. We like men making a comeback, young women are fun to play at as life, and our battles to recover can be stymied by a tough cookie of a relationship crossed. Helping college kids by testing women for quality vs. sex takes charisma. I appreciate the main character for his humanity and contributions and not for acting like a jerk to women in person. By including women and business, this genre of who is good and evil with our love of cars is more enriching than the cowboys and Indians of past Hollywood.

Domestic Violence and Related Tests for Clients
Mon, 2010-06-21 17:40

• <u>Advocacy</u>

The local newspaper recent top story states, "Sheriff's Domestic Violence Arrest Stuns the Community." The man who was reported as the dominant aggressor was an advocate for woman and children in his civic life. Perhaps in a policy to protect victims, we don't read the private details of the story. Without defending a harsh law man, sometimes women try to provoke a man for testing and control. Is he real? How does he handle anger? Are we distinct from past lives? Questions like this are in the minds of professionals and family members with the mental health system. Somebody's clients have to be on emergency alert to act non-violently in every situation and use words to resolve conflict. Understanding the emotions, foul language, and rude body language of anger and frustration is not accepted toleration in strict, unkind societies like we have today.

Critical Thinking and Diversity
Mon, 2010-05-24 23:51

- Critical Thinking Fighting Suppression

Collating information, gathering intelligence, and synthesizing opinions and describing alternate ways of thinking is a definition of critical thinking. Having freedom means expressing thoughts that can be different from others and doing so free from harm or restriction. The point of diversity in the work place is only partly to provide opportunity to oppressed workers. Diversity is to count in different points of view and finding new solutions to challenges that the existing mindset might not ever notice as worthwhile or have the courage to do otherwise. A second opinion from a different doctor or taking another look within oneself can conjure up a new avenue of care and responsibility using diverse judgments. It's simply important to think critically and creatively from politics to medicine, from perceptions of ethnic stereotypes to standards of what is a nation. We must be free of the "same page," one-size-fits-all mentality that makes the Status Quo granite and changeless.

Soft on the Problem
Wed, 2010-05-05 21:10

- Holistic Community and Perma culture

Conformity and punishment leads criminal justice for adults. A jurisdiction applying corrections with intolerance and a lack of understanding is often unfair and is not always efficient to strengthening progress. Utilizing my elected school board wishes as an official I spoke on the board against "behavior catches" in favor of character enhancing learning methods. Instead of so much tattle telling and making examples of unwanted behavior, we could reform people holistically with community supports. Being soft on the problem is great advice to develop and strengthen people, families, and their engagement with the community. For example, getting a miscreant to slow down his driving in the senior park can smartly use life changes and cooperation to increase responsibility of any aged people. Threats and limiting movement that harms a family hinders the direction we need society to evolve into.

New START Treaty Can Be People
Submitted by Gregg Jann on Sat, 2010-04-10 21:16

- Homeland into Foreign Policy

The U.S.-Russian negotiations resulting with the New START Treaty can mean more than reducing nuclear arsenals by applying a name like that to domestic and foreign policy and American attitudes. A beginning was the changing from the Soviet Union in the early 1990s. Our electing an African American President, as I have referenced before, brings Post-Structural philosophy to respect in our stretching to the limits of change. We were radicalized to a degree after the Electoral College upset of the 2000 Presidential election. Because of higher recognition and regard of people, political progression is good to the mental health community as well. Client rights and empowerment, compassion of law, and upfront understanding family interventions increased along with better medications and improved health care. This is all to my witness.

Business and Professions Code
Fri, 2010-04-02 21:52

- Property Rights and Ethics

Adding ethics laws and aiming progressive regulations are necessary to make a more moral economy.

The people leading the work of the nation need to change themselves and the systems they are part of to increase standards of goodness with our economic structures while we are in recession and afterward. Professionals in mental health are regulated to not add Emotional Banking Units to anybody's client. Our general society discriminates against people in need. Financial advisers not advocating for their client's rights wreak havoc on capitalization efforts of the stalwarts of recovery who cyclically step back. Being responsible by saving some money for retirement after a span of time on disability is on the surface a good idea, but it is not a good one if welfare rules take all the saved earnings away by forcing liquidation of assets for eligibility a second time if one's mental health recovery hits a snag. Even my private appointment with Congress couldn't result in protection for role models of marginalized disabled people who worked their way to health for a relatively brief period of time in the important health care reforms passed less than a month ago.

Hit the Beaches While You are Together
Sat, 2010-03-06 01:05

- Family and Friends

Families need to support their members. Solemn prayer does not make for fun connections that are important to young people. The objective for family time spent together on outings like picnics, museums, ball games, etc is to have good positive feelings. Keep in mind your future, and those memories are vastly important of the better aspects of your family. Remembering your youth needs to be an inner strength if your journey of life includes the long haul of mental illness. The present company and circumstances can be difficult to teenagers. It is worth a kingdom to be together with your family units in the present world. You do not know if your survival with a positive frame of reference depends on a reservoir of knowledge, connectivity, and pleasant good times of a foundation that is your family in case something bad happens in your life down the road. Psychiatric disabilities happen all the time. The Surgeon General stated that 20% of Americans suffer from a mental illness each year. It can happen to you, and plan ahead by including positive energy with your primary mainstays throughout your life that is your family.

Nicer than Social, with Attention Needed
Fri, 2010-02-12 17:41

* Motivation

It's quite possible and technical to Maslow's Hierarchy of Needs to be friendly and loving in a big way according to accomplishments in the self esteem and actualization needs. Rising up the order requires each of the 5 stages of needs to be met as you go up the pyramid after fulfilling the need before moving on the next. Self actualizing needs and self esteem needs can include Grand Parenting and Big Love in productive output like the right electioneering, book publication, or educating audiences that are important to you. Combining service to society with higher order needs fulfillment makes these people more generative of transferable love if appreciated by the receiver than someone fighting for relationships with no honor to the Greater Good. Include attention received and given, but want more and rate those who have accomplished higher order generosity of spirit well for loving. Happy Valentine's Day from this Community Activist and Management Science/(down) Writer.

Consumer Movement and Women's Movement
Tue, 2010-01-19 19:39

* Advocacy

Knowing oppression, repression, and suppression, et al, is key to understanding "non-white" power dynamics.

It is time that either the driving forces at the bottom or from the top-down hierarchies acknowledge Post Structural philosophy in the new norms helping us gain equality within selves and our countrymen. Ignoring a type is a discrimination source harming income, relationship status, and quality of life. Investing in difficult individuals emotionally and in tasks with kindness objectives will raise motivation and talent. In post-Bush II, we are striving for the limits of fairness, representation, and civil/human rights of who we and our leadership stand for. Leading change from Knowing hardship is upsetting to class conflicts and will make friendships worth love and foreign policy once intelligently accepted as the core.

A Better Goodness
Mon, 2010-01-11 00:50

- Advocacy

Being smarter than you while working as a church custodian is a movie subject. Writing is more than the spoken word in legal impact, except for the hearing need of a woman's love. "Actions speak louder than words" is true if writing is included as action. How can the ignorant judge an action? Checking in and building trust with a person will improve a person; how else can recognized leaders know who changed the world and its ideas? The goodness that is a quiet person's action can be worth a politician with a quiver intending to earn luxury, which I consider the most of The Honorable. Progress without acknowledging the leadership in mental health and education will hurt the economy, students' sense of justice, and the reputation of a nation by harming decency. Conspiracy, profiteering, and bullying can hurt someone—fairness will land with appropriate supports.

Changing Image of ADD from Appearing Uncaring
Mon, 2009-12-28 06:01

- Prevention and Health

Reading popular culture sources can be a source of sarcasm or enlighten-ment opportunities. A store's T-shirt comparing ability to remember to love and caring extends into the mainstream of media. People with Attention Deficient not only have difficulty surviving the cut in the classroom, but their spouse material, friends, and original family make judgments of a negative nature. No one wants to be known as self centered, unaware of their sur-roundings, or too inconsiderate for relationships. If you have Attention Deficient, be sure to inform your friends and loved ones of your difficulty in general focusing as soon as issues arise. Concentration and memory is basic in-tegrity to a professional image and a diagnosis. One's big heart full of concern proven by output of activities, physical presence in meetings of spirituality and goodness, and polite contributions to the interactions need to be called atten-tion to by the consumer in prevention and in defense situations. There is nothing wrong and it is advisable to inform family of your Attention Deficit once it's determined to make matters warmer in real and in image and for them to give you prompts of what they need from you.

One Administration's Change Under the Weather
Mon, 2009-12-14 02:40

- Property Rights and Ethics

To quote an Associated Press news article in the local Sunday newspaper on scientists working on Global Warming, "And they compared contrarians to communists-baiting Sen. Joseph McCarthy and Somali pirates. They also called them out-and-out frauds." The first term paper I ever created and then recycled into adult college reading from 1980 to 1982 was "Economic Mechanisms for Reducing Pollution." Is AP reading my stuff and applying it to Status Quo politicians, some lawyers, IP arbitragers, and systems like Mental Health and Education? I upgraded my ecology leanings to implement social measures as part of the world of humanity.

Something for Lengthy Holidays
Thu, 2009-11-26 09:07

- Family and Friends

The season being a source of sadness or even flare-ups of depression for many, celebrating the holidays with activities is a must for most anyone. Simple experiences like tasting traditional food like eggnog, sweets, and cider can blend with festive meal extravaganzas with family and friends. Making a point to decorate and celebrate lighting ceremonies from your apartment mantles to the civic square is seasonal treasure. Bustling retail is excitement for penniless window shoppers, generous gift givers, and busy workers. For times suited for relaxation, try January for commercial and schedule repose. Invite your brother's family for something simple at your place just for family togetherness, and start asking the invitation now and well in advance for a special re-latedness.

Law is Erroneous in Defining American Sometimes
Mon, 2009-11-09 00:17

- Critical Thinking Fighting Suppression

Born in the USA and not renouncing citizenship is basic American, therefore all ideas springing forth in support are American. The Red Scare presumably ended in the 1950s with the best hearts opposing blacklists and McCarthyism. We need ideas to evolve and lead, and greater divergence of behavior accepted. Conceptualizing independence for an individual requires responsibility with standards of freedom, self reliance, caring, and interdependence with varying ranges of action and "thought resolve." It's a conversational starter to say you're American once you can fix a bicycle (like a flat tire) and cook lyrically good Potatoes O'Brien with disregard to the stuff you and your parents bought. It's bratty to police social skills. Intend to develop the ability of a connection or rehab a business partner to gain respect in morals. Assert interventions to make a safe, secure, and understanding place for all types and generations of others and include you without expecting anything in return.

From a Minister's Son
Wed, 2009-10-21 00:07

- Holistic Community and Perma culture

Certain occupations stamp their children with significant impact outside of what is provided to them. Albeit sometimes misguided in following a set of teachings, sons and daughters of ministers can live through intentional testing by their parents, the pulpit of the church, or the congregational throngs. Getting the community to act with care and love and truth is one discipline that lacks accountability. A less passive, somewhat aggressive style of Personhood can accept conflict and punishment of the inner group more than preaching peace and kindness. A minister's son needs backing from people outside the parent's congregation to carry his mission to the outer society. Once one determines some type of ministerial nature is foremost on one's or a leader's mind it is easier to work for social justice. A belief, representation of an organization, and due diligence on the problems of the era will make changes. A life dedicated to higher order principles taught elsewhere and applied everywhere son has gone has a rock of a guide if his was a well known minister throughout the country like my late father to me—the author.

Start with One Day
Sun, 2009-10-11 06:08

- Motivation

Loving you is a key to confidence for leadership of self and to love another. Hard fought existence or challenging battles for accomplishments are vital for life satisfaction. Your daily routines are important for your stability, your future goals depend on them, and are the basis to reaching out to others. Start by "inventing" a day for just yourself and extend a routine of activities of living as full a life as you can to the rest of the week. For example, Sundays with news, church attendance, football, and an optional stroll in nature came to me with a tiny bit of practice and realization of what I liked. Work and a night out with a regular activity can make a second routine day. Use your creativity in developing your interests favoring short term with long term goals not conflicting.

Be flexible to open up for a change of plans for the day, particularly if you are looking for friendship or a deep connection.

Do Ask and Tell Nice Bigger than You See In Person
Sun, 2009-10-11 00:47

- Advocacy

Discriminations are to be fought against together and alone until we are accepting and understanding of people not like ourselves. The current debate about the military punishing gay soldiers is about discrimination. What about saying "nice" to describe civilians? Our society, as I see it, is, "Don't Ask, Don't Tell" about a person being nice. Use leadership in making our homeland secure and kind and respectful. Our citizens need to share bio-information if someone is nice more than pleasant company to his target audience. If someone is "big love" in morals and caring for the national spirit or for an individual, we need to spread words meaning goodness to that person. Friendly to a person's sexual aspirations or good company to strangers is a small part of what our society needs to give just desserts to out of kindness to nice people doing good favors for society at large.

Reform in Rewarding the Original Talent
Wed, 2009-09-30 07:38

- Property Rights and Ethics

Learning James Marshall discovered gold at Sutter's Mill back in 1848 and died penniless as a miner after a hard life is not fit for modern standards except for thievery and crudity. The Marshall Plan after WWII showed U.S. generosity and rebuilding cultures along with forgiveness. God forbid what Reagan era business college students meant with full knowledge of California history and asking an inventor and writer which "Marshall Plan" he wanted. The creator may have answered the California One due to ignorant parochialism. Reform in many fields, from authentically worded politicians to teachers developing many curriculums, is necessary to reward the original talent to increase national character, trust and a greater innovative spirit to add to the quality that is California and the US.

Citizenship for Health Care Reform One Avenue
Sat, 2009-09-12 02:21

- Homeland into Foreign Policy

Touching the bone in calling out to the President, "You liar," is a testament to feeling and logical sanity. In health care reform, unlike more conservative pragmatists, most of Sonoma County legislators believe in their heart in providing health insurance to illegal immigrants. It saves costs to reduce hospital stays and emergency room treatments for maintenance and preventative health care. The emergency room costs are saved by offering health insurance plans to illegal immigrants is money to taxpayers, hospitals, and a poor segment of the population. An honest need for Americans is the health care availability, and some feel slighted if the major legislative push is not just for us Americans. Get this need for citizens passed in Congress by writing letters to your Congressman and participating in town halls in support of health care reform. Like the growth of an initially approved small park's lands into a larger park later as an expected way of the legislative business, gaining access to health care for all as a human right that is funded is the most important thing we can do right now. The sensible thing to advocate for illegal immigrants can come later when the dollars saved to us and the beneficial employment balance sheets add up in the minds of those taxpayers thinking it is unfounded to help people from another country who live here.

My Brother's Keeper
Sat, 2009-08-22 02:36

- <u>Family and Friends</u>

Cain's relationship to Abel is a violent bible story of jealousy, regard and recognition, and murder. Eve's older son telling God he was not Abel's keeper seems to have been an excuse told to an all-knowing deity. With a different angle for more kindness in a family and more than merely keeping track of time and whereabouts that some modern brothers are too bothered to do, we in America must have adults and children to try for stronger family bonds. Protecting my brother in times of trouble and need is a true brothers' keeper that includes property, emotional bonding, and physical health and welfare. The Holy Spirit is commonplace safety of the community. Social welfare programs are justice to human rights and provide a container to those housed in programs. An adult family member needs to step to the plate and go to bat in real life person terms to assist the security and loving ability of someone who's wandered in the darkness for decades. ...with study thanks to a reverend of Christ Church United Methodist and a Rabbi of a Jewish Congregation we once shared space with.

Have Good Fun at School this Year
Sat, 2009-08-08 17:22

- <u>Family and Friends</u>

Starting right now when school starts, get off the blocks and introduce yourself to past and new people. Try new things to do and keep the old things that were positive energy to your life. Gain in maturity in a sense of respect and empathy. Be smarter in life by not hurting others or yourself in an interactive rigmarole where small emotional transgressions of each other are to be accepted. Keep a head on your shoulders and get the work of school accomplished for the long run. Have fun yourself, and if you have the wherewithal keep those feeling isolated in mind to share your fun with.

Fairness Means Reasonable Standard
Sun, 2009-07-19 12:49

• <u>Property Rights and Ethics</u>

A legal dichotomy appears possible when I read that the law and courts are competent jurisdictions. A Reasonable Person standard is important to recognize for personal, civil and business rights of individuals as well as public policy. Is it reasonably prudent to suffer for your own behavior when you know it is not popular? We lose ability as a whole when morality is not taken well by courts, is jinxed in social relations, or is punished by mass society. Empathy, character of morals, and diversity of constructive opinion are needed to be preferred traits in legal terms from health to business, from journalism to international relations. Lawyers listen to the top of the hierarchy and don't seem to favor people who are too ethical to be liked at work and in community and who don't get promoted to a higher level because of their character. A good leader extends opportunity to talents not always appreciated by himself or the individual's peers. The art of humanity doing things may be unfair to some degree, but Kennedy's Nome and San Francisco comparison is taken wrongly if people, authority, and power try to make situations unfair.

Justice, Morals + the Times We're In
Mon, 2009-07-06 15:08

• <u>Homeland into Foreign Policy</u>

The best time to make improvements in morals and ethical structures in business, relationships, and our general political scene is when the economy is performing down and I'm tired of war. When the economy is booming people are following the invisible hand of capitalism and are acting full throttle on the greed aspect at the expense of honest right behavior to do good. Sharing our home for out of luck family or being active in the political process for social justice are a couple of good deeds that reward emotional balance sheets. Progress in the homeland aimed for people, humanity, and what government does is earning the U.S.A. for what we say it means. This is opposed to what observer critical individuals possibly from other nations say USA means.

Upgrade Reformers in 4th of July Spirit
Sun, 2009-06-21 00:45

- Homeland into Foreign Policy

American history is made of success and reform. Improving an aspect of an American institution is seen as rewarding to the reformer in and of itself. Intrinsic pride and satisfaction in accomplishing for the Greater Good fits a need in a component of happiness. Paying a dollar bonus to the people who risk designing the change or promoting those coming up with the new plans may be needed to get big things done with the small, like health care reform currently. Recognizing the Patriotic trait to improve and then internalizing the result with tangible reward is fair leadership held accountable.

The Truly Warm and Moral Workplace
Sat, 2009-06-13 15:39

- Property Rights and Ethics

Winning rights does not equate to ability for kindness. We have a President to particularly address sore spots and improve national internal weaknesses. The women's movement seems to have intentionally lost nice by following competitive business roles and regimented interpersonal relations. Contrary to an ethical workplace, "Mean Party" management that suppresses workers to beat out ideas hurts one or a few employees to the company's credit. The mental health system employer is also harmful like this, showing Reagan's noted business problems of creativity and leadership. To take ideas without giving credit from the working disabled, similarly vulnerable, and those vying for promotion without providing monetary reward is wrong and lacks honor. Oppressing intellectual ability loses what we need as a nation, and we blame it on moribund unions, older workers, and schools. Much of the nation's leadership is not decent to their people who "squish" out productivity while being smothered away. An economic correction paying the right people with a promoted position is due now to move mountains in a recession.

Prancing with Zilches
Wed, 2009-05-20 17:57

- Holistic Community and Perma culture

People who are never going to say anything of critical significance can play a mean isolation game. Quiet types who speak their mind at least some of the time can be worthwhile for their insightful contributions to the dialogue at the moment. Youthful behavior should be protected socially, politically and economically from exploitation, and it follows that a reputation shouldn't follow due to fairness to the young person. The California theme of fresh starts shows understanding, but does the understanding go to advocates of people and causes even if they are not an authentic member of the movement? Talking to himself out of cognitive dissonance using words he hasn't learned other than the negative connotation of his environment needs to be known as out of place and not real. Not even delusional symptoms, venting when uncomfortable can be embarrassing but why punish the person for a lifetime. Herein lies a lesson to be learned from crudity and inhuman treatment for those harming someone from the past and that person could even have been speaking for others and acting in advocacy in testing the crowd of crucifixion.

Bettering the World: Internal Improvement All Good
Wed, 2009-04-29 18:19

- Reviews and Entertainment

A collection of public letters, speeches, and legal entries of this Community Activist spanning my adulthood is currently published in a book titled Bettering the World. Writing for print may have shown organization, intelligence, and outer-world perspective to perceived threatening forces interested in control and limiting freedom through the mental health system.

My life methods were known as "wise base running" and I kept me clear of the law and similar foibles, such as substance abuse and trouble with relationships. Take a look at the news beyond an individual. Do you see by reading Bettering the World with the annotated dates this book of suggestions could have been a needed and looked for idea for the Russian people to crumble the former Soviet Union? Elections and school board, Mental Health Services Act genesis, management and labor production, and even a feature Hollywood movie of an alleged projection of my 5% area leads a person to ponder my influences, not withstanding those accomplishments not in the book. Step forward for anyone knowing the true credit. Feel welcome to purchase Bettering the World by Gregg K. Jann at a bookstore or online for a $12 cover price. Book I out of print October 2014.

Supporting Education's Contribution Through Hiring
Wed, 2009-04-15 21:06

- Property Rights and Ethics

A custodian does not often need to speak English on the job, and it was taught to me decades ago English speaking was an illegal job requirement if not necessary for the job. College graduates can read, write, and have intellectual stamina and exploration. If a job placement likes interpersonal qualities like "bounce" and comfortable personal sales attributes, college graduates may not get a preference. Graduates are hurt if their stated idealistic or airy desired salary ranges are not negotiable by an intolerant prospective employer. The graduate has a record of supporting research growth and productive development of higher educational institutions and professors. An employer who doesn't like to hire people with a degree prevents team capability from developing and these employers do less a favor for our country.

Psyllium Seed Husks Good for Longevity
Sat, 2009-04-04 16:24

- Prevention and Health

Personal experience with a herb is expressed here in a usually opinion talk and time together blog home page in using my health services business tax license from Santa Rosa, CA. Doctor One: "We know high cholesterol increases the chance for heart attacks." Doctor Two: "Psyllium Seed Husks are a natural food that lowers cholesterol." Retired Doctor Three: "Psyllium Husks lower cholesterol up to 15%." Using the bulk food bins at natural and fine food stores is cheaper than flavored over-the-counter fiber and laxative products made from psyllium husks. Another web site states to take the psyllium husks 1 hour before meds or two hours after because the herb may inhibit medicine absorbability. Internet research suggests one to 3 teaspoons mixed with a glass of water a day, carefully depending on your ability to take something that acts like a laxative. A native plant of India, Pakistan and North Africa, farmers and no-sin-tax-here underground micro-economy can Make Laxatives Not War, a gag I said as a teenager that finally leads to paying some peace agreements.

Inexperienced Skill A Little Hazed
Sat, 2009-03-28 12:32

- Reviews and Entertainment

A bowling score of 129 by the President is an excellent score to reveal in first entertainment contexts. With the myriad of complex issues to act on, Barak O'Bama presented a side that having fun and playing off pressure is one priority of mental health. His self-deprecating manner, highlighting an example which offended some receiving media attention, sets a tone of approachability in highly competitive cultures of Washington, Wall Street, Main Street, and sports. Standing firm by respecting each one of us is important for advocates and the public alike. The "Message of 129" is reaching out and across as equals in good, clean fun for social health in our situational diversity right where we are.

Living Hardships and National Public Relations
Sat, 2009-03-07 16:02

- Homeland into Foreign Policy

Social Equity in areas such as poverty, discriminations, barriers to entry, and people needing supports in health and rehabilitation is not usually appreciated in comprehensive focused plans in ecology, business, and the interpersonal fabric of neighborhoods. The people of hurt conditions need to advocate for themselves with others, including strangers, reaching out with understanding and support to permit survival from hardships which do create a glorious history. We can expand the definitions and applications of Human Rights for our own nation's economic liking, business productivity statistics, and private living standards making an overall greater cohesiveness in richness. Recognizing the importance of the REAL behind national Public Relations described in a rival/enemy government's encyclopedia entry on history I read when writing college papers from the smallest books I could find would improve lives and broad reputations for our industry and statesmanship.

Prevailing Management School
Sat, 2009-02-21 02:44

- Motivation

From Scientific Management in the 1920s to the School of Human Relations, trends in management work evolve and methods get fine-tuned over time. I heard in 1990 from a fellow manager born outside the USA that the world wide management attitude is "She Sucked" at the end of every century of recorded business literature. This viewpoint appears to be where none of the needs of the employees are met by their supervisor's role other than the paycheck and that which power provides. Perhaps we can transition with our Government today standing for change. Best practice can be management is supportive of its employees who are creating their work place with intrinsic security, love, and self esteem, etc., and keeping their quality intact even though it's harder under financially strapped times. Domineering credit-taking and over control forced on those below in the hierarchy must be eliminated and replaced for more authenticity to the employee. Productivity could meet standards, and we'd have the ability to bear either "banana republic" style ease of interaction at work or the enforcing of robotic boundaries to keep personal relationships competitive for only those outside.

Kindness Not Withheld
Mon, 2009-02-02 19:47

- Family and Friends

Offering outward signs of emotional support or secure comfort is optionally appreciated. Underlying manipulations of getting only what one wants by either end of the channel is judged differently. A selfish interest in trying to be kind can be alternately smart, unfriendly, or perhaps gentlemanly in today's day and age, but not wise or pure. Sharing of wealth in kindness can be intended for one, a few people, or a large society and can be known or unknown. To recognize someone for generosity of spirit and love to you it is best to go deeper than pleasure of either. Be open and informing about deeds worth your best friend this month of February values at least.

Power Back Biting
Mon, 2009-01-12 15:15

- Advocacy

A manager at a mental health system employer once said for peer staff to "always err on the side of friendly." Bending rules of the hierarchy in advocacy, stepping through boundaries and trying to make friends with colleagues, or socializing with somebody's client can be professional and wanted. A friendly explanation in volunteering information can be penalized legally. Too often the inadequacy of an employer's rating method results in "bite them in the ass" performance reviews which highlight what was spoken too much over work accomplished. A more assertive workforce is made, yet self effacing demurs or calling attention to weaknesses in asking for supervision is rated low in a downward cast pro-forma for expediency. Gentle kindness and innovation are discouraged in a biased opinion on attitude. While advocating against discrimination and stigma at work is noble, not revealing one's success stories of being there is a compromise that consumer idealists should make for job security that unfortunately keeps the world a little colder.

Problem vs. Solution Economics
Fri, 2008-12-19 16:03

- Motivation

Our own economic standing is not our only indicator if we're in a recession or a depression. OK now and worrying about the future makes a tinge of bad feeling. Brace yourself knowing some news sources say any change in the economy is bad news. We still have family leave legislation, which is good news in emergency times. Welfare to work programs assist recipients with jobs and support for a population in distress were only for women last time I checked. Looking at the big picture, we can see hope in news attention to alternative energy and electric cars. Best we understand news reports are one source of reality checks and sometimes give a sense of progress in the long haul.

Customer Service to the Max Takes
Wed, 2008-11-26 11:36

- Advocacy

When needed, excellent customer service can make the difference for independence in life for the focus point of the economy. A consumer of mental health can be involved in operating equipment and systems after participating in technology purchases when the merchant offers excellent customer service. Rules against reasonable accommodations in the marketplace not based on time available of the sales force are mean spirited. The usual horror stories of a standard waiting period of 34 minutes on the phone to cancel internet service when it is not an option on the web site is punishing. A gym's code to not comply with a request to end the membership and keep charging the client until the end of the week plus 30 days is dishonest. Instead of providing hard-boiled organizational kindness with staff coaching the customer, government agencies and businesses trying to force an assignment of a case manager is not close to what we need to get a leg up for most freedom.

A Life of Abundance
Mon, 2008-11-10 19:03

- Holistic Community and Perma culture

Take Living Abundantly to mean spiritually and not by measures of material wealth. Living Abundant is more than fellowship. It is centered on love. Spreading the greater good in acts that are humanitarian, environmental, or empowering to faith are key to meaningfulness, which is a component of happiness. Whether single or with a family of your own, giving of oneself and sacrificing for others can well be sound judgment if the journey was an investment into a life well-lived. Reflection and meditative self examination of this type of living can provide checks to wholeness which can't be used up, spent, or stolen by anyone else.

Patient as Political Prisoner of Conscious
Fri, 2008-10-31 13:22

- Reviews and Entertainment

The movie Flash of Genius depicts one man's fight for what's right and his own wealth against intellectual property theft by industrialists. Being sent due to circumstances to a mental treatment facility until he gives up this fight makes a prisoner of conscience that sometimes occurs to patients today. Society treating an epic challenge to be right in the same vein as the private alcoholic's struggles results in natural consequences of fighting battles alone like losing a marriage and living a lower standard of living. This country, our courts, and the education in our schools need to raise the bar of a more ethical IP creative standard, as it is honor that wins the war.

Glastnos, Perestroika, More Moral
Thu, 2008-10-23 16:18

- Homeland into Foreign Policy

What I remember from Gorbachev and President Reagan's working together in the 1980s was the former Soviet leader stating we all needed openness and restructuring and Reagan saying, "I know we're more moral" here in the US. The field and personality of mental health care and treatment is the place to most apply these 3 traits to implement a stronger and more improved social challenge we face. We have progressed in treating and accepting psychiatric disabilities from years past. In an open thread discussion to talk and advocate in the community you are in, without forgetting mental health's current shortcomings, what personal areas and professional fields can these 3 stated qualities continue to grow us as a person and as a nation?

Roommate Law and Civil Harassment
Sat, 2008-10-04 16:24

- Advocacy

The subject of Roommate Law needs a guiding, understandable code with law enforcement back up. A funny, small time movie of yesteryear called behavior of prankster psychological warfare on acquaintances "effing you." Dealing out consequences or punishments to people whose behavior is not liked by adults sharing a home is not a big concern of "smile police." Fighting or moving on are not the only tools for independent living. The Sonoma County District Attorney will enforce Civil Harassment paperwork that is available to those not in dating relationships. It works like a Temporary Restraining Order. Justice can eliminate things like "spelunking" for the environment in taking mail invoices of a person or home based business, which can harm credit ratings but city police does not make arrests for stealing paper. With the U.S. Forest Service not hiring those that support violent activities that are pro-environment, this is a legal citation for good legalizing to make whole the victim and rehabilitate the perpetrator of stealing invoices. Prevention of "crazy making" to irritate those not liked for whatever reason requires a cop at the door with an understandable code and justice tools to stop intentional infliction of emotional distress from those living in the same home. A legally enforceable Roommate Law will also break barriers in the community through the home by making it safer to integrate the mentally ill to stop harm done of "effing you."

Trying to Change, the Cautious, and Accomplishments
Mon, 2008-09-15 09:09

- Motivation

In a squabble between public agencies, the official administering of working together creates a "lead agency" trying to make improvements and a "responsible agency" providing a foundation of status quo. This dynamic is a more cautious set of rules guiding or obstructing a change agent. This facet of organizations can be exemplified by the internal workings of the Methodist Church or the building of a new public school with additional traffic measures on the streets. In an individual's psychology, our personality shadow makes us comfortable or not with the brain stem tenet "Is my risking who I really am?" In personal life, for business, and in government, is the leader/risk worth being rewarded in merely making the effort for biased progress when the cautious authority is not persuaded to change? In material terms and to those providing income, is making accomplishments out of achievements that newly exist in the status quo of the organization a better reason to rate excellence as opposed to the Habits Performance Standard common in the marketplace?

Work (Plus) Proof for Professionals and Consumers
Sun, 2008-07-20 14:47

- Prevention and Health

Hard pressed to find rare examples of mental health recovery, a first-hand proof is success of Work Plus. Working enough for independent living without supervision is what I call Work Plus recovery, without regard to feelings in the Social Security bureaucracy tradition. Similar in a finer vein was working 2 full time equivalents (1 FTE is 40 hours a week) 2 weeks in a row, making a busy business owner who additionally spent time developing products for his own private sole proprietorship. Calling me a union sleeper with business & sales executive duties has funny connotations. Group Home

Counselor can work a day job at one bank's back room supplies the proof. Sensitive Resister social rehab counselors causing tardiness at the presentable business college graduate's bank job is one of the similar hurdles of a former consumer to those clients who volunteer-only as participants of processing recovery. By making an introductory sales quota on a month and dressing nicely while grooming at the group home is a rare combination of competence that just isn't done frequently because of the unique determination and distinctive qualifications of staff.

Chapter 2

An Innocent Man's
Rejuvenation Discoveries

January 19, 2013

Dr.
Medical Association

RE: Article on Gregg Jann's original naming of a famous disease

As per our phone and in person visits this past week, I propose a 1-3 page article on how I invented first and originally the AIDS full name and acronym as its source point genesis person while a student in the process of transferring the Chico State University. I was visiting the nice town with my mother, who drove me, in spring of 1982. We checked out downtown and the word-smithing starts with her asking me to walk alone into a movie theater lobby on a relaxing first trip. We also enjoyed and swam at a public pool cut with cement in Big Chico Creek at One Mile and I still remember the bikini clad woman with a rare directed hello from me.

I will include story for more general relating to of the leaps of faith in word choices, that I placed together the main elements of the concepts of a definitive article, and that I made up the order of the full name of Acquired Immune Deficiency Syndrome with the intent of making a sound bite that could save lives in the "catchy" name alone. The wand light emitting a definitive article was innovative to author, the management information systems major, as was the unseen poke in my stomach from the innkeeper of the theater that felt like a gun shooting inside an eavesdropping device in me when I told him, "I have a name for the disease." Could he have been a special orders person from the University, CDC, or even military establishment? Still to present, I don't know the answers to many of the questions of set up and spreading of this disease name/product of my mind as I was racing in imagination on my way home and mostly forgot all details for summer, school years, and seemed to be in a foggy haze all the while on the specifics.

I was a family friend of a past Executive Director of the Medical Association at the time. He was my first job reference when I graduated. NAB was always good friends of my Chico travel companion my mother. N knew I was original with words not spoken and that I had claim to being a Number One M*A*S*H TV show fan with no reality of consequences of my joy at rebellion. In the article I will explain the reasons exactly why I kept myself hidden all these years, primarily that I did not want pressure of fame on me for hygiene and happiness nor did I want to be a target for gayness hazards as a straight white heterosexual with little but abstinence emotional strength at 21 and older like I was running for Protestant Pope.

Mr. Gregg Jann currently writes a blog for his trademarked sole proprietorship in mental health services and does some educational presentations. Gregg Jann is a former elected official in education. Gregg is looking for more professional backup and insight to consult him on his recovery models to design, articulate, and generalize what he has worked on. Gregg Jann also wants to strengthen his leading concepts of the value of original source point genesis of many of the most important creations we have had in the USA in his time.

Jann Demystifying Affects™

May 27, 2010

RE: Record of Deposits

File for records requested

Dear Ms. D:

I'm glad to be working with you as my eligibility worker, as I think I requested your name for my normalization innocently as a saint and virgin with questions raised from Hollywood. I was an intern under you and H in the Assemblyman's office at 50 D St for a year and a half after graduating from Sonoma State in the mid 1990s.

Who can inform me on a ballot initiative that I believe I am the genesis of and guide, which resulted in Food Trucking Sales Service calling me the Best Taxer in the Nation after 2004. They observed me driving, talking, and using my own brain and intellectual ability in fighting for freedom from suppression when I was a customer service manager. I'd appreciate if you ever have the time and your rules allow for important communication from the county or state. Maybe a dialogue and fact finding state funding contacts on my behalf and informing me of my influence will get you the County Employee of the Month. I was chair of a county board and then successfully elected to a school board, so this scheme might work for you and then some.

For the quarterly record on CMSP, here is the deposit record. I am flat broke and do not sell drugs or stolen property.

Each deposit made into my checking account was the result of Unemployment Insurance income or State Disability Income. I would cash some of the check for out of pocket expenditures and deposit the remaining balance of the checks. I haven't received money from the ballot initiative from working, my RFPs, or the Marquis Who's Who in America recognition.

My $300.00 deposit into my Savings Account in May was cash on hand (Income sources noted in the above paragraph). I transferred on occasion cash that I held and turned it into Traveler's Checks for safe handling and safe keeping.

Thank you,

October 18, 2009

Dear Editor:

From your report in Sunday's newspaper, making Laguna de Santa Rosa more accessible to the public with planned trails is big progress for Sonoma County. We are breaking a stronghold in non-people interests locally. This anti-public, not for the greater good stance has been entrenched in our politics at least since I moved here in 1967.

Back in 1980 I first wrote a report creatively titled, "Economic Mechanisms for Reducing Pollution" for a student assignment. The literature review introduced to me the utilization of tax credits to curb air, water, and land pollution. I held a long-term, keen interest for ecology to include humans in environmental policy. Today, a few of our cities contain the human element in their general plans.

I built tools with non-violence as a goal potentially for the constitution from my Piner-Olivet Union School District Governing Board past times. Negotiating for mental health consumer labor rights in a union contract was successful and we can say clients have evidence in being counted as people in the economy.

Acknowledging Sonoma County to recognize lifestyle more than corporations and counting humans as humans will enhance our county in all economic turns by being authentic.

Sunday was also heart-warming by going to Fort Mason Center in San Francisco. I watched a Teaching Tolerance premier on the Delano Strike and the table grape boycott. This letter is the same message carried differently.

(Super bowl Sunday of a year some ago)

Dear Founders of Yahoo, Inc:

There is an urgent and important matter regarding the naming of Yahoo for your company. Am I a source that is known to you? I have not revealed that I think I am before this letter. I am aware of Intellectual Property attorneys and that they are very expensive and don't take on Goliath capriciously. Can you please bear with me and determine in a way I like my meaning to your company.

I authored a book written over 26 years titled Bettering the World. It's an editorial collection started in my 3-colleges years back in 1982. I had some success at the fine computer school of Chico State and graduated in Management Science after attending Santa Rosa Junior College. I went on to a brief management career at a national retailer in San Francisco before getting a second degree from Sonoma State. Then I went into a civic career while being a group home counselor, culminating in election on a school board. Currently, I own a trademarked-twice sole proprietorship with a health services business tax license from the City of Santa Rosa.

Since 1967, I was young in Santa Rosa as well as still live here. I was bi-coastal some years from my father's residence in New City, New York while he was working as a national Presbyterian Minister out of Manhattan during my early teens and young adulthood. My mother was legal secretary to the Sonoma County District Attorney's Office. Both are alive and well past the age of retirement and appear to be relaxing in late life.

Of note to both of us is that I was born in Lexington, Nebraska. It is here in Dawson County I first heard and said the word of Yahoo, meaning a country bumpkin. When I was 4 or 5 years old, I remember saying it should be the name of a company. Then on the Central Committee in Sonoma soon after Sonoma State, I called out "yahoo" to people I liked and felt that way about myself.

Can I be a noted influence on the naming of your company? Please correspond if you see my connection or you may wish to provide a better idea of where your company's name started.

I do need for myself and for others for you to see I have value in my word-choices and how I went about things. I do believe I mean justice and peace and kindness from my work and life in a principled manner I hold dear.

Don't mind my modest means or counter productive life as a contributor to society. I need you to answer this correspondence to tell me if you started from my background and creativity and words, as I feel I've accomplished a lot from poverty and condemnation. As I said in one of my speeches in my book, it's quintessential American to succeed in life after rising from difficult circumstances. Please be actively truthful to my memory and carry due regard to my wishes for a better life for me.

Sincerely,

The Honorable Gregg K. Jann, call me Gregg

January 10, 2011

Dear Sir or Madam,

In years past and starting when I was Chair of the Sonoma County Mental Health Board and continuing while being the first formal liaison for the California Network of Mental Health Clients (California Mental Health Directors Association), I participated in legislative and client advocacy. Some other positions I have held include being President of the Santa Rosa Democratic Club and Vice President of the Piner-Olivet Union School District Governing Board.

In the process of starting my own sole proprietorship trademarked in mental health services and educational curricula, named Jann Demystifying Affects at www.jannda.com, I worked on policies that lead to Prop 63. It was noted that I was early in the process and helped the ballot initiatives. I'm looking for more substantial credits that are due me.

In fact, in the recent past I was named in Marquis Who's Who in America and my biography here listed "planning and design of Prop 63- the Mental Health Services Act." I participated in weekly teleconferences with Paul Yoder facilitating and I participated on my own in meetings at the Oakland Tower at their Airport, the Sacramento Airport, and Sacramento hotel meeting rooms. We'd discuss the need for the ballot initiative, and I made persuasive arguments that just having it on the ballot would help destigmatize the population.

Do you agree I was the main force to initiate and include the funding mechanism of taxing incomes over 1 million dollars one percent? I made arguments based on Herb Caen's old column and my letters to the editor and my writings, elected career, and personal story that may have started when I asked for a ballot initiative in the 1990s.

In earnest, I wrote a voc rehab bill proposal for then State Senator Wesley Chesbro aimed for consumers of mental health services one year before Prop 63 was on the ballot. I advocated this, wrote the bill explanation, and posted my proposal for consumers to see. I also was working as a counselor for a mental health contractor at the time.

I seem to remember a phone call offering me the median income for a family of 4 in Santa Rosa to reward my efforts. I don't know who made the call and I don't do business like that. I haven't heard back from my counter proposal.

Am I "in the money" ready to receive income from the big business of ballot initiatives? I'm looking for acknowledgment and recognition, and need to know where the state department stands so I can get proper credit for my innovation and contributions.

I am requesting a credits list of who received the legislative credit and who received the money for the ballot initiative that passed. Please tell me in a proper letter and tell me where the money is.

Thank you for responding to me and my request. I'm looking forward to hearing accurately your portrayal of events that an insider should follow. Again, write me where the money is while you are at it.

Sincerely,

Tracking Influences of IP

Monday, November 30, 2009 6:37 AM

To

Cc:

Gregg K. Jann
Jann Demystifying Affects

November 29, 2009

My remembered and valued Professors from 1982-1986:

Dear SL and JM,

I am a graduate of Management Science in August 1986. I took several MINS courses like Comparative Hardware and Software, Management of Information Centers, System Analysis, and Introduction to Management Information Systems-MINS 110. I took Business Law 54-Survey or Introduction to Law from Professor J. Like many classes, I repeated my Business Law class for requirements and learned more because of the second addition, when J's class seemed like Honors Law and I learned the elements of civil disputes.

I've written SL before and I am not quite certain of any memory with me. We took a field trip to Moffett Field and Sacramento and saw a vault of molten gold being heated. My life turned more into the night field trip of JM's police ride-along however, as most of my work experience has been as group home counselor. Also have done sales, and management retail, and now just retail associate part time in this economy.

I'm writing to both of you with some success and a request for correspondence or a meeting. I'm in Marquis Who's Who in America in the Health Services Section for ethical leadership. I'm an accomplished elected official in education. I think and feel I did outstanding accomplishments dating back to a Chico neighborhood coffee house or theater lobby in Spring 1982, before I transferred from Santa Rosa Junior College the next Fall. I still live in Santa Rosa, and it's a 3 1/2 hour drive which I can make in person if we schedule an appointment or is simply a phone call better? I think I can get farther if I talk not on the phone, but if that is easiest for you either of you I can.

Management Science had a bulletin board at Glenn Hall designed by Dr. "Wild Bill" who I think was the one who put a large picture of a bomb exploding or an atom bomb exploding. I'm an essayist who published last May a book of letters and editorials written over 26 years titled Bettering the World. I wrote and include philosophy of peace and justice starting in school newspapers before, during, and after my Wildcat days.

Can we communicate between us about the picture of the bomb, what that may have meant to Management Science students and the major, and if we were discriminated by the Cold War? I feel my story and life history of successes with little money impact the foreign policy. I have some involvement in local politics and have talked to a dear friend of mine who was at Chico with me who now works at the US Naval Weapons Research Center.

I can be found on Facebook.com and LinkedIn.

I'm concerned about Intellectual Property and I have filed and defended trademarks of Jann DA and Jann Demystifying Affects in Mental Health Services with a San Mateo IP Attorney. I have these in an international class at the US Patent and Trademark Office, along with copy rights for my book, What is Mental Illness, and a separate paper titled Face Value Selling.

I'd like to discuss with a professor that I had on the history and if I'm included in the "bleeding edge" of society before the "leading edge of technology." I want to track my influences and your opinion if IP was treated like the California Gold Rush in miners living a hard life and the original talent of discoverer James Marshall dying penniless.

I'm a positive influence for wholesome forces for children. I want to know with more legal certainty if I was taken from my personal story and writing to create famous work. I believe I was plagiarized or was a victim of infanticide in others making government programs and educational curriculum, movies like The 40 Year Old Virgin, and the Proposition 63 ballot initiative of the Mental Health Services Act passed by voters in November 2004. I created "http://" before typing in "www." in a Sonoma State University computer on an unmarked keyboard after keeping my brother's secret code a secret to point to this Minister's Son in the treacherous Silicon Valley physics work.

I'm trying to say I wrote the name and acronym of a disease at the Chico coffee house or theater lobby before I attended. The disease was named by me after I read a screen from a light the size of a pen. The screen was a definitive article on the unnamed disease, and I fashioned something "catchy" with a leap of faith of the concepts believed at the time by laboratory scientists and researchers.

Please connect with me, a Marquis Who's Who member, to assist in your former student and graduate build his reputation and help the reputation of the school we are part of.

I did get a 2nd BA from Sonoma State University in Business Economics in 1994. I had an AS in Computer Science from Santa Rosa Junior College transferring into Chico State. I've also taken several courses in psychology to aid my expertise and specialty in my company in educating high and middle school students.

I own Jann Demystifying Affects with a city Health Services Business Tax license. I write a 3-weekly blog on mental health and critical thinking at www.jannda.com

Lets talk to help me firm up some of my assumptions I have of my influences. We can have a reunion of Management Science students or a general 25 year reunion of 1986 graduates. I can help this if you can help direct me. I just want solid ground to know where I and my writing affected others.

Mr. President: White House, Washington DC

12/28/11: similar and more info to a voice mail and then Contact Us webmail on 11/11/11 at 11:12pm]

After hearing the President's speech in which he informed the American people the US captured and killed FBI's Most Wanted Osama bin Laden last spring in April, I have finally realized that I, Gregg K. Jann of Santa Rosa, CA have been used as a Presidential Speechwriter and Writer by several Presidents starting with Reagan.

I would like the official Presidential speechwriter to contact me regarding my words and concepts being presented by the President of the USA.

In my book titled Bettering the World I state President Bush (the first) quoted me in his speech stating, "we need a kinder, gentler nation." I know I go as far back in time to President Reagan when I was a college student at Santa Rosa Junior College and Chico State. I am the first and original source of the AIDS disease name and acronym that I first created in spring, 1982. I was a published school newspaper writer and had continued my editorial letter collection up to and including my one and a half terms as an elected official in education.

President Clinton used my internet inventiveness and proximity without telling me he was using my words, phrases, and drawing and schema of reaching across peace for the development of the world wide web. I said "yahoo" when I felt friendly to people and repeated this while I was on the Sonoma County Democratic Central Committee. This was before the email company was formed. Did I say the gist of America Online and then get electrocuted in a doctor's office when I was a student?

I suggested Vice President Gore go for the Nobel Prize for environment and being brave in not following his President Clinton's wishes. The California ballot initiative now passed into law and is a tax funder named the Mental Health Services Act required direct work by me, Gregg K. Jann. I participated in meetings for several years and suggested the funding mechanism of taxing millionaire incomes over $1,000,000 by 1% and place this category on CA tax forms.

Obama's Czar of the Pacific is both a foreign policy dream and a mental health recovery model. President Obama's entry into the election in 08 was suggested my me, Gregg K. Jann, as a likely winner if he was Chicago money, black to make his presence improve an area of the USA, and a better than me in community organizing where I was a community activist on a winning ballot. My 2nd recommendation for a winning Nobel was Obama and he followed up in a speech in Egypt. I told all this on President Obama to my Intellectual Property Attorney in San Mateo CA.

Https:// and a stolen Peace Theme-mantic Element

When a student in Management Science taking computer software classes for Management Information Systems, I left the classroom to go to the library. I had a drafting size piece of paper handed to me for me to draw my ideas to make the computer more readable. I chose draw screen that made the computer fun in figuring out what people wanted to read. More like a mundane magazine than a fantasy cap on the head to know telepathy or something science fiction. This was in 1985 or before in the spring of 1983 or 1984. The schema was to be usefully and entertainingly informed and connected to each other, with my Peace theme making the computer better than a dictator's numbers and getting people in trouble.

I drew a rendition of electrical connections and on the right I send trending newsmakers and topical news without knowing who would source the news or make the programming company. I drew folders like we have on the right to hold information, and above that I wrote email addresses of family and important contacts for "health."

In the middle was news that was common and that you had to know. I knew weather stations were needed throughout the country, and picture images must be on the way. I studied picture elements for computer monitors when I was taking a break from Chico State.

Above middle drew lines and rectangles symbolizing the breaks and memory of web sites. I believe at this point I drew a beginning address of "http" that I knew from my family dynamics early in my life. My grandmother Bessie Hartwell said it without explanation, and so may have a sister without knowing what it means as I was going out the side yard to play baseball or other fun.

I asked my brother Scott about college requirements, catalogs, and if talking about courses was a good thing to do in college. I was in high school or the conversation was at Hacienda, because he had the brown plaid bed blanket/comforter that was always in mind. He spelled out http at this time, when I did not know what it spelled.

As far as I can gather, "http" is family coat of arms meaning silence; To not talk about this, to not answer a good question so as to create processing and independence, which could be fun, strength from fun, or strength of mind or in economic deals or wartime, etc.

Mind you, my nickname was "bug" and I didn't know why my dad named me that. It was leading recently in thinking of my Beatlemania because it was that long ago.

At the end of the drawing with some thinking delay as I wanted to come up with more, a man grabbed the drawing off the table and from my hands. At that time I felt I knew a lot of men were surrounding the inner library and if so military, I would get my money to me from trust.

In my studies I mentioned like a peer educator bringing into class there were 8 layers in computer networking. With computer science teaching bit bucket, I thought a trace and identifier could point to each computer in those letters with some other ordinary characters, like we use of:// that I may have typed in Sonoma State's Salazar Hall library or office down below from a walkway between the parking lot and Stevenson. I tried to connect with Marie the SSU business student since who I think walked with me at the time. We were in accounting and I was in a 2nd bachelor program.

On the one drawing at Chico State, I wrote some actress like ES and perhaps a not yet born EW, and threw in something to signify fake nudity with the real like an interested college student who rarely read Playboy. I did not want Censorship as it is a problem, and I am decent and more skilled at remaining so in my older, late blooming age nearing 51 this August.

I believe 2 things about my standing. The disease name of AIDS and Left essay worth adult awards, which was anti-draft and for raising the salaries of the soldiers for options of the public, were mine and hidden from view. I wanted to work in big business, and work for peace like church except not as I was a church employee for 3 ½ years from 16 to 20. I was public spirited and said things like Be a Railroad Man (SMART rail is coming soon as is the CA bullet train both passed by ballot initiative with bond money) to classmates in school or just the dorms. Those 2 things would have given me standing for a shot at making an American Peace Theme-mantic Element. I wanted a lot of money for being first and original, and the man of position doing battle like a prince. I can explain if you don't want to disqualify my battle, which the ballot proposition makes legal and more appreciation for a hard journey worth president of the USA.

At 21 I was getting covered in medicine, and I went into the doctor. It was the 2nd or 3rd time to see him, and it was a strange mass of complex. He invited me in, and I talked classmates names like who told me to tuck my shirt in, and then was electrocuted saying where is Venture Capitalists. I carried on and graduated and looked for jobs too much after.

To note about the mental health field, when I got a peer counseling job for patient rights advocacy I suddenly had a non-cancerous tumor on my ring figure. I had it removed and we have more evidence of medicine fighting for domain and control of professional boundaries and those people who are too good for mother. The Venture Capitalist electrocution could have been a friend or newspaper reader of an army buddy who wanted or didn't want my company, or the doctor thought I was getting too tall a success for him and his care.

I maintain a Peace Theme-mantic Element in real life, from union inclusion of consumer labor rights to non-violence on a school board goal for Character Ed, both first and originally like many things I have said or done.

Forced Technical Virgin is Hard Law Engineering

Not intending to get young, single, or jail convicts greater dishonesty, we as a legal society need to notice the truth of Forced Technical Virgins. It appears like someone is just lying in denying their sexual activity, and when another person confronts with charges and smut rumors a Civil Tort of Un-chastity appears where an honest victim is courageous. My business law professor in College One knew of bad people, I just didn't know who targeted "black out virgins" with so many of my fellow students around evil from drinking glory. I just had an inkling of this subject from an Italian rape report in a regional newspaper while I was a high school student. Who is more evil is not a question for only avowed not naïve or innocent people, but let's go there. We have homosexuals, women, or the defense industry who are all applicants in able to hurt someone too good for their religious shallowness in ethics. Regular men are mean about those just different as well.

You don't have to be a biker to know a "black out" can happen from lusted for activity that is probably not wanted or it can be unforced or forced. Does a psychologist know when it's good to be a virgin for courts, or is a virgin counting on his rosary too long in predominant law and order? It's a fear that the receiver of sex who has black outs or Capgrass Transference thinks the crowd knows this and says all wrongly he's gay like they're an asshole, and the act could have been his dream come true woman in a too abrupt an action preventing up to and even marriage to his one and only. He is a complete target in jail and will receive greater human rights abuses for his tight anus and convict perversion. It was naïve to say so about himself being a virgin in the commercial work of influence and leadership as well, so Church of One Kind and Law and Order rules these revealed virgins as incompetent.

University Professors say get out there for their students to be more than a text book, and civil service will not hire a virgin at all without a relationship hiding solo morality. Performance society meaning better workability is known to be sexual history for fun and glory, and stability can be attacked when someone is looking for a companion or complement socially while working. The virgin mind is free to imagine is the most valuable source of capitalism today in creativity outside of electrocution for money, for its Un-Christianity and greed of the capitalists who will not stop at anything. The businessman wanting and not pretending to be good like the Rotary of guilt money is just not civic minded until semi-retirement or the life of leisure classes. It is only good to produce what economic consumers like and need and that they will buy. The processing of the capitalist needs reform to get the origin source point person and target experience design credit and monetary value regardless if the source person is too good for current readings of religion and too moral for North American women who he wants.

A forced technical virgin can be drug induced, as we may be seeing with the Roman Catholic Church and their priest abuses. Was someone we love and don't know a drug test specimen for researching the Kennedy assassination? Was a That Someone poisoned to have strange behavior? Do they shoot ranting loonies and that type in the Capitol? The author knows nerves of steel for a time getting too close to an Auschwitz sign on a fast boat in Guatemala or the next country, and not remembering much of the incident until someone mentioned visiting Central America to see a nun/social worker. My dad was an important minister who told me a single name I like to think of and it was SG. What's an enforcer to do when the church is not a good role model from a known, leading first and where there is murder or too much sex or simply not a good family man in his own religious requirement?

Look at similes. A second or third grade student of around 8 years old doing smartly well in school with more struggle than previous. He was in classrooms being taught what he enjoyed in a boring climate of classroom friendship in a high temperature environment without fresh air of an open window. He steps out to what he looks forward to and loving the outdoors and wants to enjoy pleasant company and make real friends to spread innocently from the neighbors he said he was waiting for. His class grade of school mates disappear from eyesight whenever recess in his inability to follow their light and clothing or any part of human image as he feigned an outcast and weirdo from isolation. He was not strange and played all ways including ambition in Pope and Protestant Council of Churches to his father's dying day. In the elementary school, the man desk neighbor did his best to keep his head up and not drool from kiddie love from girls who felt sorry for the full time blind man, and looking back these girls could have intentionally blocked one direction of egress so that the PT youth who is a Kennedy Investigator must have gone that-away to a sexually blind 7 year old stud who later became the Forced Technical Virgin.

A rocket ship playground structure may still be the pride of Village school, and it remains a damned mistake to complain of being the person who is butt for chemical testing for the space program. How many brothers are too Asshole when the 60s Generation of an era have a policy for stealing something from little brother and a sociologist thinks we have a man backup from no survivors?

As the space cadet now upwards of four in stage age further trained in thermonuclear annihilation with every war movie ever made and shown during the Vietnam War, he was taught and had insight in word choices to make for interesting communication. Agreeing in calling too big a bomb an Atomic Bomb instead of a Hydrogen Weapon, and then shortening to the children in 3rd Grade, "I have a bead on the bomb," is damned for good intentions in diplomacy, peace, and business which still worth having made attempts at. That child lived and has family from his father and mother, but no women want to change the world with love for a man like a true hero. Remember, we elected Primarily a Black Man to US President before a woman who was bred from a sales manager.

A human's communication pattern is learned by the third grade. I must have made a hero from not saying A-bomb in New York/New Jersey Newark Airport later one at the great age of 14.

What is a hero of the Cold War except in not complaining they are all gone is a statement less than Gregg. Anything sibling or parent is not communist if related to healthier love for someone weakened.

Can't a kindness in gently improving the man who won the Cold War and leading the Northern Hemisphere to perdition by not being a leader in wanting peace come in the form of a one and only woman lover? Appearing falsely just a mental health consumer from poisoned workability and no modeling for no personality not too quiet deserve a Nobel Prize, things were a good idea in hiding life and accomplishments as he communicated in written word. The man was stolen as a source and hurt in ordinary income from too low a position for his intelligence but not his focus in concentration. Can women who are pretty keep a moral standard except to offer this great not yet rewarded sole proprietor their body and social warmth in a person's lifetime? Can a PYT work for his heart with her goodness and giving him hot loving for relationship with him together then easy pass to his hoped for finale marriage worth his life goal.

Song Larking and the Dolly Lama, a misspelling of Dalai Lama

Humming when I'm uncomfortable harkens back in an age regression to youthful days. Since I wasn't aware of any singing much I can pinpoint a few gems and know one rock solid snip-it that made the radio from direct words, lyrics, and tunes that I sang.

I had forgotten I hummed out tunes when uncomfortable until I reverting to this disliked habit in the past year. Some neighbors in my building elevator would look at me and say something, but usually I am left to keep on doing this. I remembered a time when I didn't think I felt uncomfortable while visiting the town that Chico State University is in when I was first accepted into the college.

I rewrote my experience through a back then hazy mind of coming up with a disease name from a definitive article from a wand light. My mom asked me to walk into a building alone, and when writing this in a memo intended for the Sonoma County Medical Association I understood people will find out I'm creative if nothing else.

Talking to lawyers, knowing they say they don't know what morals are, they will say the song is copy right. Music recordings are not what I do, and I was too serious minded in wanting world change to spend time and my talent on learning to play a musical instrument. At the early years my outlet was church, and I liked some of those songs. I never really sang much, and never learned to sing on key like I think it should be done.

Changing the World, you say, yes. I'm not up to speed at the news from black lists, non-communication, and affordability boycotts of newspaper and online media. I didn't know my team was in the World Series during a union struggle in a targeted attack on my sanity in the scenario a judge needed to talk to me, which was always friendly in one traffic Superior Court. I didn't see a game or highlight the time earlier a decade or two they were in the World Series either, and I liked the same team when they were in the cellar and went to games as a child in the 70s. Too asshole scheduling for work from unfriendly management who aren't in Who's Who like I am, newspaper boycotts on why I purchase the paper to follow my team in August at least, and people who are uninformative when I see friendliness in my coaching to tell people. The silence I call Prancing with Zilches that I received and wrote about for professionals to consider in specified cases under their care on my blog lacks one on one communication to the Head we need to talk to which is now me. Prancing with Zilches is not my own as I had no care of modeling in face to face communications. This PWZ syndrome and personality is wide, important silence similar from church persecution and family not knowing an easy talk with a Orator at the table leaving for New York, and a class the teachers didn't like for no inquiring mind. I wonder if smart enough college graduate students get Aspergers Syndrome from no emotional connections talking mind or fun as in relationship, perhaps chemically aided in medical punishment for professional not liking.

That's right, I told my Dad I was being treated like the Dalai Lama in no one talking to me one on one, and just being tested for how much wisdom are my statements that I processed from an indirect cohort of circle of friends and backing not intended for me. I was always treated like that, except on the mental health board staff after now more so as a sole proprietor with an encompassing business license and trademark who counsels and writes experiences.

I regularly was calling my Dad late in his late life. I saw the last World Series of his life, which our team won. This World Series showed in media the last time the team was in the World Series, and I never told anybody I maybe should have thrown the star a baseball back then when I was elected and think I was invited to LA for the game when I didn't know the Giants were in the playoffs. The area is unlike me in no greater kindness than myself and my heartfelt comments to improve society and pass the time with few people who know me.

Song Larking is another capitalist reform to make the music industry cleaner and not require its sources who are kids to take drugs and fuck for an instrument. I like innocence, and think a loss of innocence in morals is depressing in a small way. It is wrong to fight a union management conflict by attacking someone's morals first hand with beautiful women he can't see, all in spirit so he doesn't ever get married and his phantom fiancé ends up trying her damndest to disqualify someone who ever loved her.

I watched a regular TV show on music videos about 5 times for education on the way to Chico. The first time I watched MTV was at an unknown acquaintance's house who I met once looking for pot plants in the garden just for the heck of it for his friend. He had a white dog. After some good songs and some others, I blurted out first and originally from my heart in singing a tune with the words, "Video killed the Rock and Roll Star." I later walked once through campus and sang that line again one time. Later it was on the radio as a one liner. This song was the last time I sang a complete song making the radio, and I always knew it. I hope the crowd of crucifixion can turn its way around and pay honesty to property ownership of a source in music and movies and others, even if I get some memory reaches wrong not printed here.

The Junior Ram football assistant coach who taught stances for a day told me, "I wrote your song." It was from me larking Dreams by Fleetwood Mac who recorded in a nearby Studio in a few months time later than that. I was standing behind the backfield before 7th Grade started as I was 12 years old in practices, number 64, and just came back from a backpacking trip with my church group in the Marble Mountains. Perhaps my first August Tip to US President somewhere here? I fully expected to start first string, and from the 2nd game I was in the regular rotation and played all 3 back positions each game once I made the weight limit by dropping some on 2 apples for lunch and running. I was uncomfortable and campy like clean burlesque except in my mind and not dirty, or later I saw the Karate Kid making a strange movement. This singing is in a haze, and I think I told a girl I first met in geography class who is in my memory as the prettiest girl in class with few others. I know my Mom flipped out from too much anxiety when I simply told her I invented a song and was going to tell her singing on the front yard of a house we lived in. I know I was forced into remission into my Virgin Exoshell and not remembering my creative product of my mind as I had a lifelong difficulty in remembering what I say and sang, now fixed. That memo I finally wrote to the Medical Association brought both her and my angle to light, and it was right not for them to publish a legal threat which may be classified. It is right here in this book under my name, name including work and a better description of the man associated with what is given as his name. I was funny and psychological in Pop Warner league huddles, and in a long junior high and Junior Varsity football career I scored about 14 to 16 touchdowns, played on a winner while picking up Most Valuable Back, and intercepted passes and recovered fumbles.

I could have been further target source designer of finishing "Dreams" (after original source point larker) and other songs on that album. Maybe I'll get a Grammy like the singer/songwriter/performer in a new credit like my bill/initiative proposal shall protect. I think I'm "Imagine" by John Lennon in song larking outside a bathroom door in my own home, with sister help who I don't know which. Those three songs performed in music (not my sisters) are clear in my mind, and I wonder if I go back to 3—4 years old for Beatlemania like "I Want to Hold Your Hand." A great formula for a band I am not sure of is to get it from wholesome kids just popping it out and then with or without parents the song larks are professionally forwarded from like a quality church minister and his Music and Choir Directors. It a stretch to be a pauper from the Mid West and meet the Queen and Princes of Great Britain, and I'm like that except we have to stand in court for truth. Which being legal in civil torts is an effort for the products of mind that aren't popular. Band and groups should care well about larking credits, even if partial.

A year ago I wrote a Hollywood celebrity who I also wonder if I am titlist of her first big movie. I didn't tell her that. In my communication, I told her I was lied to like Himmler or Eichmann because of song play. I don't know which in Hitler's Fourth Reich did it like this. I didn't think of my historical songs as mine as they were playing on the radio a lot before I was nearing 21 in front of MTV. That last song is about ending creativity and free thought about entertainment and arts, and forcing imagery into a one way track-no harm ever intended.

Teach Peace and Creative Accountability as a ballot known measure may crack the case, if half truths are people who are my friends, are reformers, or just want to get things right and more interesting as we grow a more authentic social and economic and political economy. They have a book on creativity and performances not listed in public on entertainment or so I've heard, and I never asked.

I am titlist of The 40 Year Old Virgin spoken to a school superintendent while I was elected there and later on the weekend I said it again at Harrah's at Lake Tahoe on a gaming table where I took a $1 million dollar chip intending to return it to the house for further discussion but someone took the coin from my hotel room while I was sleepy; and Silver Linings Playbook complete with Eagles green, dancing, and not like me back to an early doctor. My woman doctor and I talked like Descendents which I wonder if I was electronically eavesdropped, and I know from my work I said Institute of Love Diseases for a medical training clinic and junket belongs in Mexico or Cuba for un-American images and disability images in nearly the same conversation. In college in a department of defense house I completely described a movie I saw in the theater, analogous of what we knew about AIDS less than I, and I never saw the title. Is a DH film about Northern California not The Graduate but something like Sonoma Jack Man(maybe The Monkey One if that is a title)? That is my movie, where is the life, times, and money for my credit and mind for greater creativity and production that I deserve and we are changing the law to credit me.

Where the industry is corrupt, it takes a reformer who wants his credits and money correct; or it's just the Legislature doing business as usual in making less needed changes.

Chapter 3

From One Honor to Another Honor

February 27, 2010

Dear Assemblywoman Noreen Evans:

I am seeking Legislative assistance for a constituent in receiving money for mental health education. I'm looking for a resolution that I and my sole proprietorship are valuable to the community and even worth contract dollars to place above any perceived or real past practice rules of board membership. My 10 year conflict of interest statement ended in 2008 for the Sonoma County Mental Health Board and the school board never provided one.

I own a part time sole proprietorship in mental health education and training. Jann Demystifying Affects has a health services business tax license from the City of Santa Rosa and trademarks owned in mental health services with the legal expertise paid for by me of a San Mateo IP attorney.

Paying customers are hard to come by. I can talk to schools about psychiatric disabilities in a good way. I have copy rights to a pamphlet I compiled as Chair of the Sonoma County Mental Health Board and have continued with more of my personal story and examples in a self published book titled Bettering the World by Red Lead Press out of Pittsburg, PA.

Is there a necessity to be approved by the state for me to make money as an educator and consultant and provider to mental health? I am concerned about past practice in non-paid work as a board member, at Piner-Olivet USD as well, and the County Mental Health Division seems discriminatory. I did work for 10 years as a psychosocial rehabilitation counselor for a non-profit and wrote contract language to include consumer employees in union rights with Service Employees International Union (SEIU).

Can your office make resolution for the legislature to deem my work and life experience valuable and worth money to me? I realize the budget mess we are in is hard to solve. I believe it is proven my classroom education services prevent institutionalization costs by students seeking help voluntarily and before they arrive in a police car after getting the scientific information I provide and my personal story. My work and web site in advocating for consumers assists in their recovery and the body of critical thinking aids in freedom of expression and escape from repressions.

Please help me qualify for state funds as qualified if chosen to provide services. I need assistance for my sole proprietorship in establishing my career reputation along with my college degrees from the California State University system and book publication. I made it into Marquis Who's Who in America as of 2008 before I made fame.

Also, who gets the money credit for Proposition 63, the passage of the Mental Health Services Act. I was working with Rep LF of then State Senator Wes Chesbro's office in the fall before and generally made statements to be the genesis of the ballot initiative. I submitted a vocational rehabilitation bill proposal (in Bettering the World) in October of 2003. This was the legislative season of Prop 63 in its passage in November 2004 and my ideas could have taken off from planning meetings with pertinent organizations and relevant people I was having in the immediate years before. Am I to be locked out of ballot initiative money or is adjudication possible in my favor to collect money?

Regardless of the above paragraph, I would like clearance and full confidence that I am eligible to receive state, federal, and county contracts for services performed and achievements t hat have passed to enable less stigma to mental health consumers. If remuneration not in the past, at least in the future.

For the record, I received consulting services fees from Sonoma County Office of Education and was an Independent Contractor briefly with APS Healthcare, aside from Buckelew Programs and CSN employment stints before this past Christmas. I am more knowledgeable and more worthwhile now than I was then.

Contact Us Page state assembly:

I've worked with you Michael in negotiating the first contract labor agreement at CSN when you were GM of SEIU. I was simultaneously elected to a school board in Santa Rosa and became President of the Santa Rosa Democractic Club. Since that time I was a route sales manager, and now have owned my mental health care education company since 2005.

I am writing regarding my wishes to create a "teach peace" ballot initiative. It is based on my school board goal on character education placed on the district budget and curriculum Goals and Success Indicators.

It will be my 2nd ballot initiative. The first was Prop 63 which became the Mental Health Services Act. I was involved in planning meetings and my own advocacy in creating and inventing the funding mechanism of taxing millionaire incomes 1% was kept on the ballot. I was involved from 1998 to 2002 and the early policies I originally spoke kept with the successful ballot measure held. I have not been paid by (CA)/National Institute of Health (person) or anyone for my role in the MHSA and I wanted to be. It is too much usury to be primary responsible in raising so much funds and not be paid for it. I have not even received money for my RFPs I submitted to Sonoma County that enhance services and are innovative in preventing illness and the effects. My company is Jannda or Jann Demystifying Affects with a blog on the web site at www.jannda.com.

I have copy righted the union labor section on consumer employees that I authored and the school board goad on non-violence. These are included in my book titled Bettering the World (Red Lead Press) and soon available in book stores in the USA and United Kingdom.

Compensation to me is an issue. It I haven't been paid for the MHSA in any way from my IP work and advocacy, how can I get paid for the "Teach Peace" ballot initiative I am planning?

There is a problem with acknowledging me as owner. The President used my pseudonym in a speech on bin Laden and unrewarded me.

Michael, can you help me?

March 5, 2012

The Honorable Gregg K. Jann

Dear Honorable Yamada

I met you Mariko at the SCDCC Crab Feed a week ago Friday. I was selling raffle tickets and we got into a discussion about bullying legislation. You stated you supported such legislation, and you would forward what I email on the topic to Senator Mark Leno. Mariko said Leno tries to introduce bullying legislation in the schools.

I have a couple of concerns about my piece in my suggestions for legislation. My work on the Piner-Olivet Union School District Governing Board was strongly supported by my being elected in the general election and saying issues of non-violence, people skills, and mental health education on my successful ballot statement. I advocated through Governing Board Comments by attending educational conferences in Sonoma County and career related activities in mental health. I received a Masters in Governance from the California School Boards Association. Utilizing correct school leadership principles the non-violence and Character Ed work I did set the direction of the school district, not specific hands-on, in the classroom strategies. The goal I author does not to micromanage teachers but to guide the district and hold accountability. By the way, I currently own a mental health education company named Jann Demystifying Affects with a web site and blog at www.jannda.com.

I want my work as a school board member to be the central basis for a statewide ballot initiative from my life dedicated with open minded morals, peace, a book published, and America with elections in mind, heart and soul. The non-violence as part of character education with critical thinking applied to teaching peace needs awareness so that our students can spread what we teach with the collective mood making us a better and stronger state. By a public debate on something not controversial for young students for the goal we would gain a common ground on which to build collaborative, interdependent peaceful and secure communities and less criminal acts by those who could be affected.

I believe police organizations approve of my work on the school board. By entering my concepts into the general population the safety of non-violence would spread from anti-gangs, empathy preventing harming people, and the character of anger management and impulse control in the schools' curriculum leading to safer streets over time for all of us. My goal reaches beyond the topical anti-bullying set.

I own copy right to the Piner-Olivet character education goal as it appears on the District Goals and Success Indicators document which guided budget and curriculum decisions during my time on the school board. Please offer me something if you want it in policy outside the district or legislation. My intellectual property needs to be credited worth owning my second ballot initiative. I am in Marquis Who's Who in America in the Health Services Section a lot for design of Proposition 63, the Mental Health Services Act. I have yet to receive pay for participating in planning meetings and contributing early policies that lead to the ballot initiative. I created the funding mechanism spoken verbally solely from me as original source genesis taken verbatim from my mouth in meetings that is on the Easy Form of California tax code for 1% of incomes over \$1,000,000 going for mental health enhancement and innovation. I want to be paid for the MHSA for my contributions and for these related proposals for non-violence as key concepts in school governance overseeing the curriculum pieces selected for students and community. It is fair for me to be paid well and would make better students who believe in justice economically and socially can result for idea leadership for me whether recognized or unrecognized as of yet by the state or counties for work I've done in word smithing and conceptualizing.

From a ballot initiative for teach peace in the schools we could spread to adults a more nirvana on earth spirit. A related idea proposal for a Peace Treaties Park in Mendocino, or near Santa Cruz or somewhere else for families of residents normally to hike and camp and to encourage interaction and agreements of private citizens making foreign deals internationally affecting business, medicine, exchange educations, and international dating security for a good native time. Don't foreign influencers love our bears and redwoods and the preservation ethic of the western states?

Please acknowledge me for my letter, leadership and efforts for a teach peace ballot initiative, crediting the idea person of both this non-violence goal on state and federal constitution and the MHSA funding mechanism, and a Peace Treaties Park in California. I want to be paid well commensurate with my influences originating from my talent and it makes a more authentic economy to remunerate me now. Continue the discussion with me so I can lead the teach peace I have worked on locally.

Alene:
Did they or we spy on me? Was my story of my experience used?

Gregg Jann

—On **Thu, 11/10/11**

Subject: RE: Teach Peace - credit verification asked for
Date: Thursday, November 10, 2011, 9:22 AM

Good Morning Greg,

The United States Government is not awarding the $25 million nor anyone credit for the capture of Osama Bin Laden. The information leading to his capture came from electronic intelligence and not human informants.

Best,
Alene Seward
Office of Congresswoman Lynn Woolsey

From: Gregg Jann
Sent: Thursday, November 10, 2011 9:19 am
Subject: RE: Teach Peace - credit verification asked for

Alene,

From a separate action from Lynn and Congress be acknowledgment and reward for my namesake role in the capture and killing of Osama bin Laden? August Tip is the name I gave to a Farsi speaking Private Investigator who is American. I gave a plea and received a different call. The PI and I were looking for a pot of money for me from the Cal ballot initiative Prop 63 design and planning that I did for the MHSA. We discussed my counter beliefs for peace, the DA style solution to war, my conservative sex values, my visits from the middle East and Pakistan on my company's blog, and I turned in my money to her. My Grandfather and WWII killed Uncle are named August first or middle.

Tell me what you know about Gregg Jann and August Tip, from Congress to the President, for a stronger Peace Department resolve.

Gregg Jann
Jann Demystifying Affects (tm)

Application for NOW national advisory committee

Thursday, January 6, 2011 12:10 AM
From:
"Gregg Jann"
To: NOW, Washington DC
Message contains attachments
    1   File (16KB) <u>NOW application.docx</u>
Gregg K. Jann

P.O. Box 4207
Santa Rosa, CA 95402
Home
Email
National Organization for Women application:
Global Strategies and Issues Advisory Committee
Summary:

1) - NOW Member since 1999
2) - Endorsed NOW Candidate for political office in 1996
3) - previous legislative committee experience in California and election victories in local races
4) - Consumer mental health expert recognized in Marquis Who's Who in America 2008 - 2014

I'm a general advocate and am particularly strong in mental health. I own a company and have written a book de-stigmatizing mental health and providing hope.

The issue I propose for NOW and this Global Strategies and Issues Advisory Committee stems from my experience in the psychiatric disabled. 30% of the world's population is mental health consumers that I heard when investigating if I should run for US Congress, and 20% of Americans will suffer from a mental illness in their lifetime.

My view on foreign policy is to compare nations by how we treat our downtrodden people, as in women which does not block generally lower classes of comeuppance. In biblical terms, a Book of Mathew's "taking the care of the least of these" would improve lives here and abroad.

I am accomplished in working for underrepresented populations. I am a former elected official in education.

Please look more at my letter of interest. I'm looking forward to hearing from you soon. You may contact me at the address listed.

Sincerely,
Gregg K. Jann
Jann Demystifying Affects™

Chapter 4

The Goal in the States for Mental Health

Teach Peace ballot initiative - Is it worth U.S. Constitution, the California State Constitution or State Law leading.

By Gregg K. Jann /Draft One was written Earth Day 4/27/ 2013

TEACH PEACE and CREATIVE ACCOUNTABILITY

HONORABLE INSERTION to be INCLUDED in FULL as part of BALLOT INITIATIVE PROPOSAL:

The State declares we are all humans, and each person worthwhile whatever is the ME of me; each I differing of my own names, styles, images, knowledge, skill sets, and quality. Interacting from one human to the next may improve me, and striving for better society and world is also a Goal presently for Initiative. Valuing more people inclusive not ownership all.

TEACH PEACE is not controversial for young students, and good Governance lets teachers teach according to them. This ballot proposition is based on elected school board work currently in place for teaching students on the over-riding budget and curriculum foundation locally derived at Piner-Olivet Union School District in Santa Rosa, Sonoma County. The POUSD piece was written by a single Governing Board Member who advocated for character education constantly to staff and his fellow board. (During which he was a counselor for paid work for adults in psycho-social rehab, currently a sole proprietor.) The Governing Board passed the article unanimously in natural timeline following 9/11, keeping our course we started in '98. With head start and heart up, the Student Education Goal completed for student and district teachers about 5 years after a first statement adding to a common theme while in Southern California for a California School Boards Association event. The Character Ed Proponent on the Board who designed this ballot proposal began open meeting, Brown Act in force, Governing Board Comments and conference study in late 1998 after his election. The District withstood the test.

Character Ed Proponent on the Board designed the TEACH PEACE/non-violence as a ballot initiative for a good faith discussion and actions of students and all adults to accept non-violence into character, which grows an appropriate level to grade of social and emotional maturity for children and some adults who are affected, and for the adults/parents to lead our communities safely at present until TEACH PEACE/non-violence tenets spread more for all adults and children for all time. The Initiative shall endeavor to make a kinder, gentler nation of the USA and complex in what we can do for supports. One example, the POUSD has adopted anti-bullying policies and program because of local enactment of the goal that is imbedded here in this Initiative proposal. TEACH PEACE tenets prove students wiser in dealing with conflict, isolation, wholesome friendship, and other quality our teachers taught.

Character Ed Proponent on the Board addresses through TEACH PEACE ballot initiative in part seeming to be creativity and leadership problems in California and the country. Greater ethics, and Project starts with an idea; we need to know who the person is origin and recognize and pay for. TEACH PEACE recognizes stronger the SOURCE of endeavor intellectually, government legislation, entertainment, and in business and overall the STATE will gain more authenticity in economy. Our students and parents and interested adults will increase in competency because of the better honor of starts and morals gaining recognition both valuable and invaluable. Let's count in the people for Original Source Point and Target Source Designer who are individuals for new credits on starting the value later added to for creative endeavors, businesses founding, and enterprises like movies and song larking. Talking the people of ideas expressed, and specific viewpoints used.

TEACH PEACE has a relation in income and credit through disabled property rights worth value currently denied mental health consumers, and which TEACH PEACE enhances generally for the creative public and negating competency restrictions that make for untrue sources of ownership away from children who start unknowingly or disabled who can't usually keep. One motive for TEACH PEACE shall make more social and economic justice for the state's creative and leadership people in government and private applications by recognizing more roles to acknowledge and require the payment of money to source at the beginning point and in target design. All adults, regardless of relationship status or age or disability file, shall have property rights worth income and credit when their expressed ideas and experience are utilized because of their person or their work. Rights of ownership and credit and income for Original Source Point Person and Target Source Designer acknowledging the human element that is the people we have/are, regardless of liking who started the enterprise or endeavor.

This ballot initiative recognizes enhanced programs and services worth funding from the MHSA in sources and recovery. The Governor's Millionaires Tax can help spread non-violence throughout the community. State government reform projects in recognizing ideas and letters from constituents who create original value or new counter plans if suggestions took hold. Legal recourse of the citizen reformer can take to court for money in the bank for intellectual property theft and fraud for falsifying accomplishment of a participant in policy, or in any Product of the Mind by a Source in a jurisdiction accepted State funding, e.g. Chico State U., work groups for computer popularity, etc. Legal action and consequences for dishonesty to the original source or source target designer can have an impact for the citizens who like authenticity and for the victim who shall be paid value regardless of party of the source, making government an improved ethics in code.

Consumers of disability needs, participants in mental health services, and clients of vocational rehab shall be defined as people, for lawyers in commercial law and for marriages included. The people regardless of needs and disability possess property rights and ownership rights of creativity and income and credit from their own contributions due them, as well as their job and/or career. Proposition highlights one way up socio-economically for creative talent regardless of age, relationship status, or disability file. Other methods shall exist. This is intended contradictory to slave-like statuses from vocational assistance in place and time. Voters yes support positively TEACH PEACE and accomplishments and an authentic economy and better social interaction. Voters Yes want finishes to the exchange in CA ballot law: WH Candidate sitting President quote, "Indentured Servitude like Independent Contractor is fine" for recipients who have in place property and salary caps and condemned outside of court never able to earn enough to re/pay in full entitlements, medical care, and housing. Ballot proposition shall recover value for Source from non-credit and takeous advantageous of the legal creative type persons who are Proposition's subjects within state jurisdictions. Unethical conduct toward excellent source designer participants and these victims of IP fraud/theft shall have legal remedies paid; require action with a Court appointed attorney and prosecutors so Source can profit and have alleged or actual "loan" forgiveness of all safety net programs he needed in his journey of life while denied being credit and hurt in income from earned salary. Quote to Back to BO: "Like I told you about. I'm O Source Pt of the alias/pseudonym "August Tip" used by you in your speech on a Spring Sunday in 2011 on the capture and killing of FBI's Most Wanted. I told you on voicemail and by your Contact Us web site on Veterans Day in 2011. Where is my FBI reward money for my Peace motivation & communication. States Rights Peace Plan in DC and for economy? CEPotB may know who helped his part with Jannda.com paying one contract. BO do your part for him."

It matters to "TEACH PEACE" that the State affirms a more authentic economy from before college level at the Universities while people are students and for all adults in intellectual property rights to value. Where creations are both owned and credited to source once determined honorably and honestly, regardless of age, relationship status, or disability file. These products of the mind will be illegal to take without pay and credit or steal for whatever reason by bureaucrats, professionals, people of organizations, their family members, people on the streets and playgrounds and yards, or anyone administering the spread of talent for gain or for nothing; enforceable by civil court without time limitation and fines/jail.

The state recognizes an extreme, illegal and immoral usury to not give credit and income for raising very much TAX REVENUE that is 1% or more of incomes over $1,000,000(MHSA and the Millionaires Tax), transforming health care delivery and then never tell the author/advocate affirmatively it was his plan the State used. This ballot proposal condemns the groups who received money and some of the credit for the MHSA for sending someone into a dire condition who was close to success and participated in design meetings only later receiving denial by departments in mental health. SACRAMENTO, et al, shall apologize with money and make whole victims of this usury to scale of the revenue generation for the government services and reforms set in place and the work that was maintained and funded. (college internet theme too) The Target Source Designer(or O Source Pt Pers.) of the Tax Mechanism used in the MHSA and which is the precedent for the Millionaires Tax, both passing popularly in election, have Designer who is Character Ed Proponent on the Board providing Intent Nexis and Legal Arguments for the tax revenue to go for TEACH PEACE programs, people, and curriculum.

In economic trade visits and international agreements, and among people that care, The State can improve comparatively among nations if this ballot proposal is passed to TEACH PEACE. Educating more inclusive topics to students, greater care in adding rights for disadvantaged, and increasing the size of income and credit of an aspect of the creative type will naturally lead and make more authentic the economy of the state. Educating students TEACH PEACE/non-violence will bring forth a wiser, more peaceful community of children and the adults therein. The Business and Professions shall add creative facilitation to client and ban comments to harm medicine.

Voters YES for this Ballot Initiative called TEACH PEACE stand for: Property rights for each one of us citizens, regardless of age, relationship status, or disability, is recognized in this ballot proposal and ownership is encouraged well taken for the person who has starts and morals in idea conceptualizing and word smithing of themes, titles with descriptions, and schemas; and even song larking the beginning of lyrics and/or tunes. These property rights of Original Source Point Person and Target Source Designer are for all times where the vulnerable can take up a civil litigation with extended statute to anyone stealing in any organization or form of foul play. Source rights specifically directed by self to a business or professionals office certified where the disadvantaged go for a trust relationship and trust is expected wisely enough to get the word out. The original source point or source target/designer can be explained as gathering up strength and steam to take up his idea after setting it into action like I was compelled to and didn't expect a need to protect myself from the doctor I visited while a student in college. We shall recover value taken by others with this law TEACH PEACE and make more American the people of a type of authentic creativity or counter productivity.

The limitations imposed on dollar value for certain safety net programs are not addressed in this ballot initiative. Creative talent and ability to recover individual utilizations is method for upward social mobility for a legal creative type we use. Whether one's philosophy, organization, and hierarchy is worth history and progression for America depends on needs for the whole and authentic origin credit; like Spiritual Benevolence for Self based on on Maslow's Hierarchy of Needs for one business motivation model. Both students and disabled have TEACH PEACE/non-violence tenets and policies toward them as for all adults. Taking in the little people and the most disadvantaged is TEACH PEACE, where there's merit utilized this is compensated, special and/or unique contributions not barred, making more authentically recognized society and economy.

Pt of order: Medical consequences or medical punishments of any intent of the informant, derived from community comments from strangers, acquaintances or family without permission told to the medical profession and allied health care, shall be banned. These community comments are banned in health care delivery of services. Medical Punishments in the form of intentional consequences by doctor or staff for direct patient care or indirect administration, or offsite condemnation shall be illegal on "good" people, while feeling non-condemning and non-judgmental toward our fellow man. Medical harm on purpose to patient by training, those on order, or just because of greed of the doctor; utilizing dentist, doctor, medicine or allied health care through consequences for disliked behavior, whether it be: in office, in public, any convictions out of court or misdemeanors in court, or Americanisms, or relationship status, or just so because he's a consumer of disability entitlements like Medi-Cal shall be illegal and punishable by fine/prison and held liable for damages. Licensed behavior correction providers like social rehab counselors may, if that is their job duty on the spot, be the only counselors/facilities where intended consequences are legal from staff and these consequences are not chemical punishments to mind or body. No one can use shock treatment, chemical poison or any medicine expressly to punish for attitude or behavior of anyone because of politics, income, religion or duty; even to Teach Peace/non-violence enthusiasts.

Designers of student curriculum utilized, and Initiative designer who is Character Ed Proponent on the Board shall be paid for each and wider dispersal of TEACH PEACE programs/curriculum design adopted, strongholds of TEACH PEACE/non-violence currently utilized, new curriculum, or innovation for education, or teaching parts proven uniquely insightful to American character. The money from the State to make this ballot initiative proposal law is from the General Fund tax revenues, and related revenue categorical to teachers, mental health services (MHSA), and public safety (GOV'r MT '12).

Gregg Jann **TEACH PEACE**

Creative Accountability;
Property Rights for Who Creating Products of the Mind, including People with Disabilities (Business and Professions Code)

A) Both as an individual and the collective of persons of us (as in care holder trust with informed consent), who are natural people by birth, vow, and health; or those of us made good today or supported on-going by Professionals, workers, medicine, caring supports of family and friends, and the similar assistance expected for the young, aged, and disabled at some points in our lives; are recognized for having civil and economic property rights and ability to own his own creations.

    a) All individuals, regardless of age, relationship status, or disability file, possesses property rights, including intellectual property rights and career possession and real property and personal property and others, worth value monetarily, protection, and boundaries. This includes Character Ed Proponent on the Board, who is Gregg K. Jann of Santa Rosa.

B) People who have disabilities or are recovering from disability do own products of their mind in all cases, even when undergoing medicine and chemical treatments or are entitled to government benefits and are receiving supports.

C) All individuals of any degree of interdependence, relationship status, and disability possess their ability to earn income and receive un-earned income, create wealth worth value, and rights to gain recognition socially, to add and keep good medical care; especially now for implemented ideas, services, and products created by and for original source point genesis and target source designer with his passive and active participation and output in roles, talent, memberships, governance, human service volunteering, positions, supervision, conversations, or creative throughput like copyrighting by him or others who engage his experience for truth and production. Incompetent or un-qualified people may keep and grow value from their inception point if product of mind is original and creative, like we all have the rights to do so with this proposition.

D) This law acknowledges communicative facilitators into the source, and the assistance in good faith of spreading from the source with his permission and providing appropriate supports and guidance depending on worker, professional, or peer like a friend (or any person using the property from source). The property in and outside of Hollywood music and movies (i.e. Sacramento previous ballot law or Silicon Valley companies to name big value withheld at present) can be documented or undocumented intellectual property, "verbal copyright," real property, personal property, intangible property, career holdings, family wealth, and spiritual loyalties and oaths each worth monetary and emotional values to beholder and the source point person.

    a)   The Courts shall determine criminal sanctions and civil liability of the people, organizations, and groups who knowingly take the source property used for profit without informing the clients, or the vulnerable populations. The people who are used as sources who are victims of theft and/or fraud by not being informed in an understandable process for the source person do not need to have some kind of disability file or be too young for the source to have legal recourse.

E)   A "verbal copyright" by Original Source Pt. or O Source Target Designer (similar) is acknowledged and recognized with value negotiable. Persons admitting disability can own and profit from their input and experience if unique, creative, or simply implemented for ideas as a contributor to the purpose of the group, enterprise, or endeavor. Off-site quotes taken from source point person, experience viewpoints belonging to source person for specific insight, and/or management of the contributor in organizations or care for one/many all make the contributor source "too close to success" and this contributing source is an authentic target worth monetary value and for profit gain regardless of past practice of ordinary labor or unpaid work, whether the effort was nearby in the chosen field or the person attempted to or de facto was bringing in to the endeavor his experience and talents.

F)   Legal remedies shall be made available for inception points we see, read, hear, or infer experience specifically from the person we know directly or indirectly from officiated meetings, comments privately placed at home that spread away, and blurting out wherever youth play anything, where we draw, sing, and study or invent first and originally in full or part are all adding value and worth money where these creativity happenings are spread, managed, published, produced, or ghostwritten by Performer or Organizational Hierarchies and Structures. If person or his products of the mind are relevant and conducive to commercial or in productivity inherently useful, the State will factor in Source Point Person's uniqueness, first and original in successes 1 or more, and a history of output in creativity which may be published, and Genesis in starting strong/weak with the ideas and conceptualizations are factors taken in part for evidence and proof, and can be unlimited in time to collect each pot of money when Property Recovery begins in earnest by person or with his supports who may be professional or legal.

G) Forwarding rote memory and noncommercial lyrical statements are encouraged for each of us. The ballot proposal does not disallow any money a consultant with experience can raise money if authentically original from his product of his own mind. The consultant's creations must not be derivative of a client or source point designer without informed consent and at least credit, money negotiable, for the source and target specifically.

H) Recovery of property and credits to Source Persons, or any adult missing property, whom is a client/consumer/recipient of mental health services or treatment or Medi-Cal beneficiary, and the emotional making whole along with the values in monetary terms, shall be an approved as a recovery service for consumers from the Mental Health Services Act revenue generation and/or Medi-Cal or other categorical or General Fund.

I) The State shall celebrate Upward Social Mobility is possible for any citizen or adult and America is designed to be good at it including this ballot initiative. The practicalities of getting higher socio-economically are not scoffed at by public bureaucrats and treatment providers. The USM life plan or luck may not be spitefully withheld by government agencies, health treatment, or government entitlement benefits.

J) The state shall have forgiveness of safety net programs for a zero sum cost to recipient once he earns or received enough money to commendably get off entitlements of immediate benefit times. He can live alone, together with roommates, or with family for a form of limited value adding to consumer and entitlement beneficiary

K) Treating government provided human services and indigent medical care like a bank making indentured servitude of welfare recipients, disability folks, or just out of luck Medi-Cal people for making them pay for safety net or denying inheritances to and from the recipient is illegal. The safety net bank for recipients shall be condemned in the past and forever more made illegal with apologies for past practices.

L) Medical, dental, and allied health care may not provide or dispense medical punishments for consequences of patient behavior or attitudes that are dis-liked, are un-Americanisms, are due to patient convictions in and out of court, or a failure in income, politics, religion, or duty. Community comments from strangers, acquaintances, and family without direct patient permission are banned in health care and related professions and allied health for patients who have medical care to take care of them. Community Comments to Harm Banned in all Business and Professions by code and practice. NOTE:

Homeless outreach workers can perform their occupation with client rights respected. Licensed counselors can do behavior modification or rehab for inappropriate behavior, but not by chemical, medicine, or electric shock treatments that act like punishment. Possible Words and People Processing for heart, mind, and soul for behavior, feelings and attitude recommended, business and computer irrespective.

M) State Programs and Services for Sources who are persons in recovery from disability, and other services/programs related to this section, may be funded in full by the General Fund required eligible, MHSA, and other categorical, and Medi-Cal.

N) The people of the ideas expressed are the Original Source Point, same person expressing the idea if utilized and spread is the Genesis from catching on by the effort or funding. The Target Source Designer is the person who is the creditable viewpoint used for the original of the endeavor and ongoing for project. The project can be in part of many parts contributing a finished product, it can be in mainly the whole, or its entirety. It can by a theme that carries forward the invention taken hold in specific.

O) Students don't have to be competent to graduate and to own their products of their mind. Independent of class assignments and outside of projects for University is ownership capability for anyone who is source point or target source designer.

P) Ideas from idea men who conceptualize for profit or to be useful to society are kept separate in law for the person who has the ideas from the person part of harmful thoughts of crime and injury. The behavior of a creative or potential creative who seems outcast SHALL NOT BE subject to commit to mental institution or required as an "outpatient" when his mind judgment for strangeness or treatment for limiting mental thinking and experiencing for creation by medicine if not a danger to self, to others, or is gravely disabled; treatment for the Creative Person to feel and live well not denied or may even be encouraged. With this TEACH PEACE ballot initiative proposal the State recognizes American creative process and it may be tough experiences to funny men who may be children and for the too quiet introspective to get outward in ordinary personality. The state nor medical profession does not try to create and may prevent in college and graduate school cases of Aspergers-type inwardness and the harm to the mind, body, spirit, and soul or for anyone attending or working for school from no thought provoking emotional connections or medicine consequences to clients attending at some point.

Q) Invasion of privacy may be necessary for treatment of the vulnerable in our society, not in every case or for their whole life in what is supposed to be a soft way like in parenting. Don't treat adults like children. The commercially used ideas, themes, and projects gained from or utilized from a specific source may be in a "hold" or drawn from for the client or student, either/both for individual taken from, and communicative facilitator during or after the fact shall inform the source target in a timely manner as soon as possible for someone suffering possibly with leading ideas of the century like entertainment economy in the USA do. {One here with a Great American deserving that is a 49ers and others fan who categorically denied a crush on Kristy McNichol(9/11 B-day) when I heard stated while a 14 year old freshman, "you'd make a good President." This Initiative understands there are good lies yet economy can be hurt for unethical credit and attribution, there remains good philosophy in coaching in thinking everybody is not Dot in regression analysis of management science class as a Wildcat.} If legal currently to withhold someone, the People who take the idea and the ones taking and possessing stolen property will be punished in jail/fined until full disclosure and title to earnings and ownership of ideas is paid in full/or in agreement of his entitlements best/is deemed humanitarian or justice served upon any individual. Terms client/source/target are negotiable for immediate payment, or the person/victim is informed on the what's and when for reaching status, health recovery, or a just an age.

R) A "FIAT" by the state legislature or relevant Capitol leader can pass this ballot initiative named TEACH PEACE and CREATIVE AC-COUNTABILIY for reasons of enough support among the electorate, with opposition or status quo dangers to citizens who have a moral imperative to pass and possess the rights contained for good of the residents. Threatening to commit to a mental institution or truncating career and job income of participants(not an inclusive perception from reality), even if protections seem outside of Civil Rights laws temporarily or the opposite, who support the ballot initiative process with their own opinions in agreement enough calls for strategy to pass and fund TEACH PEACE. The Governor or we can ask the President of the USA to state TEACH PEACE/non-violence /CREATIVE ACCOUNTABILITY is American as "apple pie" or more so in the campaign or once accepted after election.

Gregg Jann 2013 **TEACH PEACH**

TEACH PEACE Education: (Ed Code)

A) Each District in the State shall hold accountable Teach Peace in budget, curriculum, and programs the goals and success indicators for the students in public schools—and will create and promulgate Teach Peace core over 6 grades between Kindergarten through 12th. (1/2 of grades). Private schools shall pay Character Ed Proponent on the Board who is Gregg K. Jann for their use intended, like the public shall for those programs utilized.

B) State standards shall accept changes both for academic and non-tested curriculum reflecting the Student's understanding of interpersonal skills, history progression and consequences, and mental preparation for students to later develop their own identity with TEACH PEACE content and non-violent character.

C) Curriculum, administrative policies, and programs and services may assist a safe, comfortable experience and a feeling of security of the student learning environment. Classroom education is best decided by the teacher and their professionals who direct them like the Superintendent, with an elected or appointed Board making a Governance Team providing statutory citizen direction and not micromanaging the classroom.

D) The District shall encourage student learning opportunities in non-violence, social skills, character education, and general emotional well-being. Programs may affect the entire campus culture, and include formal instruction in which students are required to participate. Staff will give reports to the Governing Board four times each year.

E) Communication to parents and guardians on Teach Peace subject content and programs/services offered and covered in a rough outline before the school year or before unit taught is optional, with the statement students are fine for this focus.

F) The State of California needs parents and interested adults to participate, as do students in spreading a peaceful, non-violent character throughout our society to be attained someday eventually as our goal.

G) Competitive sports and exercises in intra-murals or inter-scholastic, even ROTC if approved by the school board, shall not lack luster and non-violent honor in their Scholastic Body & Rules preventing of injury and insults.

H) Peace Maker Discrimination is banned in teaching, including State Employment and State services on Peace Faith and Action or gun enthusiasm if teacher/students are appropriate in conduct outside of comments. Teachers and students can discuss peace/non-violent topics delineated or in tangential without punishment. Curriculum specialists and experts and finally The District with the Courts can determine fair, free expression is utilized at the instance in time and accept in the classrooms and on campus: the people with a kinder, gentler creed to the news making, of recognized religion if not outspoken where prohibited, conscientious objection to war status seeking is legal to do, advocates of world environmental ecological systems, comments for any political side of an issue, and Patriotism support toward non-violence are all acceptable at work and in school in an not all-encompassing order in education. Students and adults with carry over idealism and newbie peaceniks can enjoy life, liberty, and the pursuit of fair trade and happiness along with value for property.

I) Designers of educational programs and character education curriculum pieces of TEACH PEACE will be paid in full, more for utilization in depending on how many students, schools, and districts utilize them. Character Ed Proponent on the Board who designed TEACH PEACE ballot initiative will be paid as well equal to one year's salary per annum per each of 58 counties.

J) TEACH PEACE programs affecting the safety of the community by staff and peer educators or just a better group of people improved by the Initiative, and non-violence curriculum are eligible for Governor's Millionaires Tax funds meant to be used for safety in the public and public safety service. The MHSA may provide funds, and the General Funds required eligible and well as categorical for education.

Gregg Jann 2013/TEACH PEACE

NO HARM TO TEACH PEACE/non-violence ADVOCATES and ELECTIONS AMNESTY (Administrative)

A) Upon starting of the ballot campaign for Election Day for this ballot proposal, the State shall declare amnesty for all parties in the TEACH PEACE campaign for those who do not commit physical hurts or any illegal harm to voters.

B) We declare TEACH PEACE/non-violence is American and wiser for students, and we should be grateful with this particular ballot initiative to have more recognized right for quality.

C) Not anyone can harm the Medicine, limit career property, add social slander, write libel, harm business income and property, take away personal property, and further remove income and credit like mentioned above for Character Ed Proponent on the Board or any of this Initiative's supporters. The individuals, organizations, or "on watch groups" who are anti-TEACH PEACE/non-violence shall not sleight or harm or otherwise infringe any rights author had previous to or after to this authored piece was shared in the community. Freedom, home, comfort and security, good environment conducive of a good wife with enough morals and looks, and maybe or not a good job can be handled and paid well and that of the supports and caring we need for a human named herein Character Ed Proponent on the Board are deserved for Character Ed Proponent on the Board.

D) The state shall provide protection of life, limb, property and health insurance and care of Character Ed Proponent on the Board.

Gregg Jann/Teach Peace 2013

REVERSE USERY and naming TARGET SOURCE DESIGNER or ORIGINAL SOURCE POINT GENESIS for Money to Origin Design State Revenue/Funding and this TEACH PEACE/non-violence Initiative (Administrative)

A) Gregg K. Jann of Santa Rosa, CA will receive credit for designing at least his 3rd ballot initiative/proposal immediately and will receive pay and credit from the state for the MHSA ('04) and this TEACH PEACE Initiative as determined by him and for his own leadership and influence to be determined on the Millionaires Tax, which was on the ballot November 2012. Character Ed Proponent on the Board set the precedent of the latest popular ballot Millionaires Tax with Prop 63 in November 2004. The state recognizes Character Ed Proponent on the Board's role in designing the taxing mechanism of the Mental Health Services Act in advocacy and perhaps his experience viewpoints in work and life and volunteering some and for his career in business, supplying legal arguments in using categorical spending on a million dollar income tax bracket(other additions to the court as we offered), and suggesting the Maslow Higher Order Needs Hierarchy in the highest of Spiritual Benevolence toward our own happiness in applying our person to our underprivileged class of people or just not-strong or the too young.

B) The money to Character Ed Proponent on the Board designing and therefore passing Teach Peace and other ballot initiatives separately will be comparable to Jarvis/Gann's take on 1978's Prop 13 in excess of $2,000,000 per annum for one initiative proposal; and added liability of 3 times for delay and denial and plus times 3 thus making 9X overall for the criminal level heart of theft by public trust/bureaucrats/organizations/unions of SACRAMENTO of Character Ed Proponent on the Board. That Prop 13 defunded the State and reduced services, while the author's talent, work and experiences added revenue and/or delivery to CA.

C) This ballot proposal declares too much usury by Sacramento revenue agents to raise very much tax dollars off the designer who is Character Ed Proponent on the Board and sending him into suffering and oblivion while denying his participation and worth of his contributions officially. The state will consider in the future to hold money in a Holding or Trust with friendly draws to Source depending on, much as Jann Demystifying Affects wants to hold value and grow the property of persons who are disabled with Character Ed Proponent on the Board the owner.

D) The state shall fund Business and/or Government liaisons shall provide advice, support, necessary operations ability and strategic planning as deemed useful; and this service shall be made available to complex plans or business people who have merit in peer run enterprises or any source in recovery. Scope of practice can extend at times interstate and globally in all areas of contracts and sales and request for proposals, with preference to original source ideas taking hold or those who supply and fill a need. Assistance does not require the Source Point Persons or Target Sources to have a disability file or a relationship status to make efforts on property recovery.

E) Payments to Character Ed Proponent on the Board for effectiveness past, current, and future in statewide program and implemented government revenue generation are applicable because it would be fairness and proper merit based on wide dispersal and in a sense of social economic justice and our need for upward social mobility to talent used in our society to improve our state of California grandly.

F) State and Public financed research funds are available to colleges and universities on TEACH PEACE/non-violence subject content from the State.

G) Freedom of expression in all peace/non-violence forms carries into hiring Academia, encouraging intellectual explorations, stretching that is not dangerous to individuals, and enthusiasm for counter to status quo shall be accepted and welcome in academic employment.

H) Work spread by politics or related marketing to civics from origin contributor's public service jurisdiction/district is to be paid consultant's fees for use in policy, setting up program, or exemplifying for curriculum to the origin, whether elected official or appointed member or an applicant for position voluntary or paid.

TEACH PEACE/non-violence WRITTEN AND PROPOSED TEXT BY: Gregg K. Jann

Gregg K. Jann   residence:

Santa Rosa, CA   Santa Rosa
Jann Demystifying Affects™ **TEACH PEACE**   Jannda.com

Item c) page 6 is © by Gregg K. Jann, Toward a Better World published as Bettering the World, April 2009

Specifically "Ed Code D" © Gregg K. Jann, Toward a Better World/Bettering the World, 2009

TEACH PEACE and CREATIVE ACCOUNTABIILITY © by Gregg K. Jann/Jann Demystifying Affects 2013

No part of this text for ballot initiative may be altered, changed, or adjusted in value without express written permission by the author.

PERSONAL: The author, original source point, and source target designer, is Character Ed Proponent on the Board, says he is alias Presidents

August Tip, and is named Gregg K. Jann by birth. He is a Democrat. Add note: Writer Gregg K. Jann is owner of a business with trademarks and copyrights in mental health services. He was a Community Activist on the ballots for successful election to non-partisan office in education and the Central Committee. He has 2 bachelor degrees in business administration and business economics, and a computer associates from a community college. He was a management trainee and assistant manager in retail of a Fortune 500 business now headquartered overseas, then counselor, appointed office, and sales executive. Gregg negotiated and set a precedent in mental health consumer labor rights in a contract article in his taking part in founding a union. Gregg suggests a Mental Health Treaty and contract world wide so Gregg can do his work on his sole proprietorship and continue his power after the campaign in a light schedule. He is author of a letters collection with a sales paper inside, and blogs at jannda.com.

Gregg was a creative type by Graduate State University training. Initiative may bring life to him acknowledging he's a bachelor who likes women and is a Protestant advocate who seems to mainly just sit in church uncomfortably. He's lived in Santa Rosa, California since kindergarten.

Born in Nebraska to a minister and homemaker/D.A. secretary; he is in Marquis Who's Who in America, Health Services Section currently in his 50th year. The on stage performance playing while Initiative was written on Earth Day and the following week was Legally Blonde, The Musical. He likes walking, nature, viewing sports, and sibling trips.

Jann Demystifying Affects™
Santa Rosa, CA 95402
www.jannda.com
Creative Origins Advocacy©Gregg Jann 2013, Jann Demystifying Affects 2013

Chapter 5

Museum and Hill Running

Civil Rights Results and Repast for Income

I'm sorry for cussing and slurring in prior entry.

I wrote my big Civil Rights result that I invented in part, and I was not acknowledged or rewarded except asked to pay more money than I had already during one campaign only. I performed work for issue positions and campaigning over the phone. Author only uses the poetic license of attention getting language to shock for the professionals in office to get them to move for me, which is true or listener doesn't know Author at all. The reader should see more to me, not less, in what I can express. Being ignored as the main USA Presidential MO creator for many administrations long over decades must wear both on the macro economy and the person at the source of his administration who has feelings. Both better for others, but how wrong is it to hurt the authentic source? Property seems ownership denied for enslavement while income discriminated in amount.

There is a solution, which is talk to author in kindness and pay writer his values in principle for Author's creations for a lot of ownership that belongs to author for his economic gain- the prescription of an elected community activist with business pedigree in health, retail and more than one college degree in business and economics.

It's a rough spot on Maslow I had in the past year and now fully there hopefully temporarily on self-design repast and recollection of memory once lost. Punishing Author is against the health care set up he asked for to gather in memories and accuracy. I'm sorry if I offend anyone like some isolated "you" case is made into by people he improved.

Hurtful Swearing Defined Psychologically

Cussing and slurring in attempting to invent a black USA President while passionately using poetic license trying to gain lucky breaks from an Intellectual Property attorney finally registered with psychological explanation while writing my 2nd book. I felt anger, embarrassment, suffering, and frustration on the streets.

Recently I bundled up 3 slurs used significantly: n-word, asshole, and act-hole; all heard first from media or during an innocent youth. Self reports to lawyers appear to punish for consequences of asserting freedom of expression. Drama in asking social favor from any professional plus intentionally defining need for electing sitting Mr. President when I generally described him unknown in 2005 stands 2 Christianity Opposed.

Considering the theory of the narrows of Maslow Hierarchy of Needs in my life in ongoing Stages work, downward force appears: 1) Results Deserving Kindnesses, and 2) Creative Processing Demanding inherent and extrinsic values below to me.

New Health Care Coverage Referral Sites

Health care is completely important. Gaining coverage is essential for pregnancy, pre-existing conditions, and prevention at least at age 40. It was vitally important to pass the Affordable Care Act of 2010 to extend health coverage to more people, as it is almost a human right to have good care in a basically wealthy nation. Have something to show for your wealth is taken as whole country of people, and good health is basic. Our society is better for our overall social fabric than a President saying with his conservative heart, "Recession is when your neighbor is out of work, depression is when you are." It is a limited view to say the economy's condition is only up to yourself and all others are meant as "screw you."

Health insurance sign up starts October 1st. Enroll at the following web sites for coverage starting January 1, 2014 if you don't have insurance.

The federal web site for the state you are living in is: www.heathcare.gov, In California its: www.CoveredCA.com

Strategy a Plus, Manipulation Unhealthy

While serving as Chair of the Sonoma County Mental Health Board, I verbalized my own insight that was funny and apolitical that in the department, "staff strategizes, clients manipulate." I'm embarking on that journey even today after the Head 90s statement in a public meeting to discover that what I stated.

Caring only about getting whatever you want anyway you can, with hitting off anything looking for immediate payback; by deceptive means and illicit motives without regard to ethics or progress to what we as a society need, is perfunctory addiction and substance abuse rawness and detrimental behavior. Upstanding civic responsibility and straight forward communication creates a planning and working mode to gain trust and this style of ways is strategy over dishonesty to connect emotionally for whomever.

This formerly employed peer counselor utilized his persuasive job coaching, unwelcome by the MH System, in Pin Ball Wizard Becoming Aware of his career pursuit and lover ship, winning hard knocks of bankruptcy, mood attacks, mental turbulence, and social isolation legislated for the Board and his own GIGO, to perform social rehab. This one survives with earnest playing worth war that he enjoys each present moment like never before and tries to recover himself who went places and created the greatest changes we have ever witnessed for the general social health and goodness of the consumer.

Leading Managers with Accomplishments

Getting more women into management and in executive support affirms different types of in person emotions to possibly connect with those workers fighting and struggling like a knight for change. A take charge leader going off tangentially from his main directive to accomplish a new innovation can be challenged at this very being, and question his sanity. People of Influence with ideas and making changes usually go too long without recognition that he did these things. How many have not yet received remuneration for the developments that were his idea while he earned equity by sweat or position and these changes are now standing tall within the status quo?

It is ordinary to block, deny, and mortally attack a history maker in jingoistic manner for unasked for goodness to the greater social/economy. Let's reach out to our change agents of business, government, and the non-profit sectors and thank them monetarily and tangibly. Reward those who made us develop our persons or organizations, fine tune our processes for recognizing people for what they have done and reward them for making a difference, and pay these people back until we pay as we go for the future like a royal commission. We need to give our due to the idea men who created our world and started true the accomplishments earned by his and our toil together, however smart he ran the work. Is this new for inventing managed care?

Counting Animals for Motivation

Coming back from 9 days in Wyoming and Yellowstone I have spent significant vacation visits protected in the wilderness. Counting animals are motivation for further visits to places preserved for us. Counting animals that are unloved by you for a project with practical purposes such as in a confusing flock formation can be daunting and lose one's interest in serious environmental considerations. Bucket lists from childhood reserve pools of some of the best visioning for places to go and things to do for kindness people and outdoorsy types (2 classifications for wilderness employment.)

Seeing animals you have never seen before can be a lifetime endeavor encouraging the best in life in simple terms like calm meditation at their site and to complex issues like transportation arrangements.

Themes like entertainment, exercise, hobbies such as photography, traveling, visiting people, exploring, history stories collection, and taking in ways of life different from the city life add to perspective in a human's life span in the rugged (rouged) individualism common to the sparsely populated regions. The animals you wanted to see added to your perspective, adventure, spirituality, hobby enjoyments and self reliance and even more resolve to face fears.

American Achievement Not Only Process

"It's podunct to not recognize an accomplishment" is advice to gain skills to honor those people and workers that made a difference. This can be a new management philosophy for the work place to support, honor, and pay rewards for the people who made innovations and resulted in changes that now exist in the industry, organization and even community environment. Generating tax revenues and inventions and programs from legislation are direct relations to success. Knowing a person is "tall" in achievements is ripe for social love of a man or woman by their intended or wanted partners, particularly if a professional attitude is present. Fighting like a knight or prince for legacy and improvement and cultural fame takes talent, stamina, and tools. Denying accurate credit of the origin, source target designer, and intellectual viewpoint of the person's resolve is wrongful banking institutionalized. Bring love to "knights and princes" in struggle for authentic innovations.

Take Ginger Ale for Stomach Sicknesses

Ginger as an ingredient in food and drink has medicinal purposes, besides masking the flavor of medicine. Ginger started growing in Asia, and has spread to Africa and the Caribbean and is primarily used as a spice and in tea. The popular soft drink Ginger Ale and Diet Ginger Ale are good for stomach problems. This soft drink makes things taste well at any time, and digests easier than colas for one. Copies of this type of soda don't have ginger. Dyspepsia and vomiting can be treated by drinking Ginger Ale, and osteoarthritis pain can be reduced. Mixed or indeterminate evidence supports consumption of Ginger Ale for muscle pain from exercising, hence athletes may be observed drinking this beverage for sore backs and worn muscles. Ginger Ale is rated not effective for colds and flu in general.

From an old wives tale I heard from my mother in Lexington, Nebraska. Cookies and prescriptions aren't wholesome to author like emotional support and kindness in a clean, goodly way using oral language and touching nicely with hugs. Rx noted online sources after author already recommended solution to Kaiser HMO staff and clients and his people from youth.

Emotional Economics

Emotional Banking Units were described in smash best-selling author Stephen Covey's 7 Habits of Highly Effective People. I remember riding the train to a sibling's house in Washington from California while first going over the workbook over a decade ago. Going onward from the book, treating people like an account leaves out a person with psychiatric disabilities, by him needing too much in not reciprocating enough equal emotional energy as he is wanting to be receiving in relationships. He may be unable to take in emotional love showing too much personality, either by overwhelming his register or by muted affect with an inability to feed others in measure of the kindness he received. I didn't say the person with psychiatric disability doesn't appreciate when people are kind to him. He may not have a way of showing he cares like the sender commonly understands easily. Habits freedom arrived to author in breaking Developmental Disability mindset quality 1 way. By looking ahead for memory requirements and predicting events before the day just arrives, we can be smarter in who we are by internalizing new habits.

During a second night shift pass on to the next consumer staff counselor, I lend a different view than my own take on Happiness Science. Freakonomics is doing whatever you want, and I see our free market leading that type of consumer psychology as well as controlling your own work. When I was a peer counselor/elected official in education I was selling "Bettering myself, improving the world" for needed direction both inward and outward in jobs, relationships, and general society. My quote is one of those things reminding me of 4th Street tabling in Santa Rosa downtown.

Get Smart with Overkill on MIS

Getting human support with instant telecommunications and a secure physical space will allow Management to go directly to the receiving end in the hierarchy for a feedback loop. The Management needs accurate reports to make quality judgment on real and perceived dangers and exceptions, or it's like P.I. details of Maxwell Smart in the 60s on television.

Denying direct feedback to Management for him to read the signs of the environmental conditions to reveal resulting actions or to understand correlation data takes guts at both ends of the communication channel. Receiver end may lose his job in top-down politics of communication breakdowns. I love theories of management too much to practice union softball like they did in this no regard symbiosis where I was a leading man. MH System still does the disjointed flow to their Santa Claus designer. Analyzing for intelligent solutions in a communication gap requires an awareness of the surroundings and presence of mind so that one can surmise and draw out the happenings of who, what, when, where. This style is reasoning backing the business organization using inferences and can be sound logically.

"Why" is a priori applying knowledge and experience to determine causes and to assign fault. One" how" in business is DSS methods utilizing probability of events to forecast initial values and the recurrences to develop outcomes via computer software.

Telling different points of contact an item of information needing feedback as we process reality is another line of communication structure to gather in the environment. As the ends of the channels of communication waiver in positioning and the feedback loops differ in things to be aware of, the items filtering through the surroundings from different foci points will be a "snap to" line of at least 2 variables correcting each other for best gauge of the bottom line truth eventually. The analysis pertaining to the very same item with the deposits of info spreading into different backgrounds is to be collected together and gathered into reading one focused point for a resulting decision.

Today's police reports and inner works remind of the rough times in Business school life. Labor unionization struggle at a mental health system employer leaving behind signed work contracts is not appreciated for earned victory in history making of the author. Thefts, un-crediting, distress tampering, and suicidal behavior of others had preparation mostly at Whitney Hall Chico and less much at the Sonoma State I graduated as well.

Lesson unknown is to not get a boss who only works to control all things work or when supervisor has a domineering demeanor on individual receiver needs/wants ala Maslow the Mean Way. A Master of Governance from the California Schools Boards Association guides the principles of leadership to not micromanage the end site of professionals and customers. This prevents over strict control and complete usury of a human for his needs by management.

The Mental Health System statewide and county has been in a non-specific individual shut down instead of granting land to this former line staff counselor/Businessman owner of initial design of tax legislation. The proposition he worked on passed the final balloting enough to succeed by a vote. Is there a Capitol for us, the people, to make better the one person who is the Man with No Name more remunerated with a greater amounts of money value for his talent utilized that changed the state/nation? Official theft of A. Designer may be compounded in the economic business cycles with the speeches and programs of presidential administrations for election to hurt aim hard like the medicine, law, and computer fields.

By the way, my degrees at 2 California State Universities plus a graduate certificate help what I do at Jann Demystifying Affects. My Santa Rosa Junior College Associates gives me time off to enjoy after starting off well with accomplishment in life and transferring. All 3 schools I honor return to me for too small amounts and are unethical for regard at this time in our history.

Small City Slip Returns to Silicon Valley in Training for Work

I'm grateful for the exercise grid at the conference, in plans to share as Peer Mentor. I delved into my 2nd legislated recovery period for a new look inside and to develop my presentations for this organization and for myself at Jann Demystifying Affects.

It was a form of sadness, not in anger, to struggle from feeling unrewarded from all the differences I have been making and kept away from joyful or just importantly meaningful engagement.

I have a 2nd book up for copy right which is a description of a new look at our Country's important advances in many markets. Feel "loser" about something money and phantom fiancé replaced Soviet style, method is to write a book and be constructive however indirectly I guess. Say "loser" with my accomplishments not to mention brand new car, and correction is more concrete as I soon bump my head after slipping on the street.

Was this word choice an instigator during a recent CAT Scan experience on a stroll with my sister once back in Santa Rosa? Wondering if sister was using "suspect kindness engagement" to misquote my blog a ways back at www.jannda.com, as many both successful and less so wouldn't want me to state this legislated quality which is untrue to me. I shouldn't have reported myself with such vulnerability when usually I feel satisfied over doing Greater Good in a big way very well. I was chuckling at the challenge to change my private world's environment when I reported this unrewarded impression at the Mentor training for check in. I decided to respond to events in my thoughts and feelings probing an updated view of my 2nd recovery time span in my life.

I feel grateful for the Mentor training check in to state some of my achievements and tell the group and facilitators that "It is podunct not to recognize an accomplishment." It is mental health field in CA, region where I live at least, business degree, management title, etc. where the best policy- and real work- producers in Sonoma County are rated on smile, relationship, and other processes of likability and not productivity resulting with innovation for the economic good. How can we reward achievements?

I think the area of property and owning creations of mind is an area for my sole proprietorship as a side of recovery that hasn't been addressed. A person making big influences and accomplishing grand things for the betterment of society needs recognition, support and economic reward. My hope and effort for myself and your organization with Sonoma County Behavioral Health is that there is reward those who do just that with merit pay for design results. My disappointment is the State has not yet credited me for design of the MHSA, and which I have made all things possible to this organization. I want to be rewarded for my policy contributions that started and formed the ballot measure that created tax legislation for incomes over $1 million. The Mentor Training made understandable my motivation to get these things right implementing economic justice to me, as I am not giving up.

Just building ability and offering a forum to help others with knowledge gained is a great feeling to share, and with an opportunity to facilitate a good class where we are for recovery is worth fine credentials.

The Honorable Requests and Conversation:

June 6, 2013

EM,

I sent off my ballot initiative proposal and entire book of ideas and concepts meant for money in a co-aligned goal of public service that is used professionally in mental health and for my own company to make and have influences in my state and world. Remember me going to the state Senator's office and talking to you at the door about an international treaty in medicine and the punishments of un-Americanisms and so? I compiled a blog since my first book on editorial letters and wrote some other letters and comments in support of my theme of crediting Intellectual Property correctly with ownership to money.

The US Copyright office should receive my hard copies by Monday, and I would like expedited processing so we in California don't miss the point of owning Peace and rewarding contributors no matter who they are, not only just the teachers who are curriculum specialists. The proposal gives permission to design social skills interactions and critical thinking of counter movements for peace in the long run of a country's existence and changing strengths to fit the societies we are and need to be and need to add with.

It fits with the Department of Peace Building proposal by Democratic Clubs with my career in adult social services to rehab people instead of incarcerating them so much. This Jann Plan for Creative Origins Advocacy proposal adds monetary value to encourage the spark of creativity and peaceful solutions like outreach and company employment. I see parallels that I may be an influence in the resolution for Department of Peace Building during my works through writing my thoughtfulness and explaining myself to US Military in town and crediting my products of my mind at the US Library of Congress.

Is revealing myself and the history in coincidence, and asking a congress rep if I have been spied on by nations, worth a Pulitzer? Did family and church leadership help found the Letters to the Editor section of a non-yes-former New York Times Newspaper named the Press Democrat or was it not that humble a start with me only riding the wave as a news carrier, elected officer, rabble rouser for progressive business, and contributor?

FYI: I know my ways seem like b.s. and ineffectual for little money to add in giving to politicians who aren't interested in good ideas, planning, and thoughtfulness; but I spread love and accountability reform like a Ministers Son. I was a tourist in Vancouver and asked a clerk there to nominate me for a Nobel Prize in Peace or just Medicine Fall 2012 unofficial pass. I have talked and asked about it with my medical sources here locally and at JCP when a seasonal employee suggesting to have a big and tall section right in the store.

Some things are intended funny as truly possible, like the man we need me to be, successful in hope and in visions for peace. The title I provided for my 2nd book currently being delivered in Washington, DC is:

A Jann Plan: Creative Origins Advocacy/Teach Peace and Creative Accountability Initiative Proposal.

A writing award named the Russian Aleksandr Solzhenitsyn is for an unliked life or something in some kind of prison of Gulag restriction like Siberia while being a critical thinking winner by the written page, maybe misunderstood to be un-American while adding to the definition legally and medically what it means to be a Patriot. I'm trying to invent this award to be given to me as an entrepreneur in mental health services business.

I just ask for a lot of money, and with a title maybe the state can accept to me Royal benevolence from countries who think I am, The Honorable. One who helped the weakest while hurt and did his assistance like a "Saint" and Virgin-of-a-Type lately read and This One contributed to the richest things on the planet too.

Does my suggested 1 or 2 ballot initiatives counter a movie peace plan that gives Hollywood rights that aren't real to the weak of who we are? Or for that matter anything creative in show or exhibited in the military except abusing magic meant for peace in our own selves? Let's talk, E, if my ballot initiative proposal(s) counters an existing peace plan or executive order anywhere in the copy right compilation of self authorship.

The Spy I Didn't Mess With

The college dorms looked mean to me after I went to that lawyer. My fellow Knads were threatening to close my major, eventually closing after I graduated. I did get the degree I wanted but I ended in the rough adding to my classes in years. To answer closing threats and prevent just for me, I walked into Chico News and Review's cover story seriptitiously(clandestine manner, unknown in a lot of ways, sneaky, not telling anyone much information about it, surprise maneuver once revealed, like a virgin State secrecy, acted wise quietly, not outward evenly to every man, intentionally confidential) to find the subject I was looking for. I paid entire monthly allowance from New York to the Most Feared Lawyer in Butte County about the University's fraud blocking my management science degree. I never followed up if paying him meant my ideas expressed were protected in my name as I wished and hope for. "TBD" in values is what I stated to a dangerous story's headline above this paragraph.

My problem is I don't know what others do and expect good trust back to me. I showed the lawyer I was recruited to go to campus to study computer science business with my world philosophy and Methodist backing through employment while at SRJC. I kept open the degree offered and expanded courses in my career objective with MINS classes by telling the college Business advisor more about the Theory of Information I was learning on my own by thinking about coursework.

It seems there are chances and risk to entering the observation and in pulling out the growing amount of data after setting up formulas and processing of the record log. Two sided probabilities of many factors and variables combine for utilization with a function channel dividing up work in breaking down the problem. Experienced seamlessly described in real time in computer connectivity like networking and the internet. For example in my life, in the Hands On observations end the colors coordination on the street grunt of a person adjacent with more than one shade to the eye required together to form sets of data sent at high speeds to greater amounts of sample field collections applied far out there. The leadership end which is a distant look can be, for example, infinite coordinates in physical outer space seen by many in front of national camera brought home for all those reasons we developed the internet (for fun, relationship, home banking, education, health status and questions, etc.) Information Theory grips the conversation of an MIS student as called attention in that meeting in a home based attorney locally 300 miles from my home. Mr. John B said the Attorney General would pass out subpoenas and make the lawyer and I travel the state for one courtroom battle after another. I paid by cash on the barrel head as he required of this former student who may be the Man of the Hour this point in our history for the Peace Department and those things I want with just dedication of a life.

I did inform the BAdvisor of the lawyer's visit. (I told people in classes my ideas about probability, observation locally, and space on the internet to not mind your stuff out far away-and read similar in a primer published 25 years after my undergrad school written by Christian Bach, PhD. I loved it. I am a big indirect about stuff I may have said in school and else, in repast wonder if what I said is mine if ever spoke first brought up later like experiences that may have happened with no immediate recall of them at first. Store bought degrees no less can be rejuvenated and refreshed as above. Accuracy is vital in crediting worth academia, and is hope I carry for money ideas where credit in business to the idea person has been unimportant in bottom line results from the bank.) I guess the B-School Advisor and I felt I was either business like in responsibility or election hopeful in developing my leadership in this way of keeping my classes and offering more of them. I threatened a tarnished reputation with a college print journalism career to expose inequities as I alone advocated for improving systems for peace efficiency right in the campus professor work in my education.

Back in the dorms, someone hit my door hard late in pitch black darkness with only the hallway lighted. I stepped out and avoided a strange weapon on the floor made of metal. The Chinese man sat cross legged and stated he was a spy.

The conversation started when the man said it was best for me to kill him.

I thought one of 3 countries and it could be a large number of nations taking my money through the use of guile and force. I stated something to return money to me when I am ready after more development of the computer world wide web, for the time I negotiate for the value of my computer role.

This spy meant this to me: I used non-violence and owner belief he needed me to keep on producing real improvement as figurehead for the internet when Peace was needed past the dictator's numbers on people and just money crediting. We needed philosophy and politics, and I am an alternative star option perhaps long gone opportunity or we can fashion more together from this work. Peace would decentralize individuals like we are people and would promote freedom from oppressive control and work conditions were to be less domineering.

I didn't feel dead as I carefully extracted myself after telling the spy the deal was later for my prior and in-processing work for separate/together gain. I knew I was unique and there's a catch to economic leadership not just in Capitalism among men and women who take advantage, crime present or not.

Russia now that you changed back your name from Soviet Union like I wanted you to retire, China who I thought California could lead with friendship, or my college buddy's Navy meant the most to me if done right need an agreement to count me. Because of who I am, I didn't really think the spy was a fraternity prank. It was mean some in the dorms with too tall a big timer in the midst, and them not ever knowing who the main influencer was, a too solo friend.

The spy could be an inside job to an industry false to the start.

Hiding Creativity Good for Form

"Wrong to judge - wrong to hide" seems 2 progressive Christian Methodist to me. Hiding creativity makes a person seem stupid, as much so as developmentally disabled ala Asperger's Syndrome in an office examination by a non-professional. Is this dumbness to others person using appearances or does he himself limit his thinking ability too much with no interaction that he can't recover from his isolating devastation. When his surrounding loves don't provide care and attention of even conversation to him, for him, known to him; he shall live with blunted affects. A heart from him can be full of life and care full of love when he can focus his attention. It is wrong to not model before him, either conversation or in happy facial expressions. Hiding his creativity for years takes strength, and this is a source of character if his mind means something of value to someone else in money and grows his own abundance of spirit in co-aligned activity. Reformers in Capitalism and/or for Protestantism struggle with being underestimated. Abject poverty denying a person's ambitions through discriminations lives longer than a dark and lonely night as per Paul's notes in the Bible. A fuller life with love bigger than you see in person waits for a power surge of their own authenticity noted for rejuvenated energy in economy and within persons.

Picking Me Clean Stealing

The evil of Picking Me Clean of taking property without paying me for it are reasons for starting wars. I may want to at least shift the thrust of war to the nation-wide Right-to-Steal of the typical barbarian mind set since before time as in the sacred catechisms. Can we end war if too much is stolen from me and correct when we are ready to win the damn thing. Maybe even foreign countries do cooperate in theft, is open for more respect to the World Equation to hold and pay him, the victim who needed health recovery as ok now at copy right. Better the example we are experiencing is the wrong false religion of stealing too much from anyone, any one person can be what the world is doing for criminal justice worth absolute hatred correction in War.

Perhaps we can prevent future wars if we can solve combat with a silly principle to act for the one redefining the law so WAR can be done and ended completely. A good plan is to utilize a new Customer Service/Hold Economy to pay the author with kindness, understanding, and value for justice to his creativity. It sounds silly to pay an American to solve the problems for one we ignored. How much economic and social and health raping does the Country/State/County jurisdiction need to pay financially to the individual target or source to correct the harm forced on him and accepted as an injustice. The Silly Principle in trying to make war obsolete or more detrimental to the remaining standing of the countries, or it can improve both countries in win/win sides to strategy of the common. This S. Principle can be marriage, one of Royalty like in past, those conditions for subhuman or gay changed to include more ability for in facto marriages of independently financially comfortable and in society, or just many people recognizing marriage—just probably for the first marriage for first time freshness peace/piece.

For enemy attacking us, one alone and fighting for his stable empire in post analysis was the final straw of the in development of the movie signifying vast rape on an underrepresented force for authenticity in our peace loving ways. Civil action to make source rich is Not Punishable by Country USA for how commonly it works, that was ordinary IP theft for family with a personality disorder under the category mental illness of a family member all denied too long perhaps. Truth is the "gem" theft of creative product starting was not ordinary people but rather corruption of industry that caused worse wars and Great Recession than we knew for the complete non-sex, non-gender wealth, income, social, health raping worth poisoning of an innocent not conceptualized and not homosexual. We kept up stealing so much from some one person weakened except for his own talent, ingenuity, and pluck with the MHSA that was passing tax legislation into existence for health. The public bureaucracy, the unions, the management of lobbyists and non-profits and California and its counties, the association people all harmed the Man with No Name, who is The Work Author who designed many things and is this Book II author.

Crashed Hurt for that Healthy Feeling Moment

And Author Background:

Author's own Pink Collar labor group home counseling employment seemed desultory, yet was sexy in love and productive outside in related legislative work and his own elections; his time in Blue Collar commission work as a trucker food salesman was double long hours, normalizing, and fun jokey; and while White Collar Senior Assistant Manager in retail, big in Christmas/otherwise, he was crossed in San Francisco by Sacramento afterward and also Capitols have been unethical away from his person when as sole proprietor and in his board work for not noticing properly with money to him.

Businessman/counselor/elected official/inventor who started from Chico State University business school with a student print journalism career set out to try to change both the work place and community for a greater good in Christian spirit. His power at grad time was based on his word smiths and drawing, and the local area discriminated his employment. Author was less aware of his life history for long afterward (until journaling after written work started in earnest with medicine titration to bring back bad times for creative capture lapses.) Economics degree added from Sonoma State University later, a few years after the first.

In his 20s, author didn't feel his strength from weakness nor would he ever expect 10 years of careerism in mental health as he did in his 30s and 40s. He feels fortunate and appreciates the small measure afterward for doing wonderful spirituality throughout his public service and private social service production.

Jannda.com writes with experienced attitude while wearing many collars and delves into a small bit of industrial psychology with re-memory on inventiveness worth USA all. We in this nation must prevent his quiet, dissociated manner from continued harm and stop theft from capitalists and others taking extreme, unfair advantage making things very aggressive and unethical to origin points.

The USA must not martyr author by refusing his needs met; through economic injustice to him, relationship discrimination forever for author, or adjudication the other's wrong religion to not-love/harm to him who is Jann Protestant or the first mainline churches. Jann Protestantism started in Presbyterian Church, USA with his national minister father out of New York and shared 2 generations with mother in local Methodist where Author began a young church employee and rabble rouser in his music. As a youth, he was shy socially out of Exoshell. In high school, He spread church teachings on protesting for natural black African mother's milk for their children and heard from his teenaged workplace CCUM minister during draft counseling he sought that, "the church supports you either way you go re: The Selective Service."

Gregg talked Protestant Religious Symbol as a young boy starting by asking about the origins of the names of the mainline denominations in faith and was true in banner church social responsibility in hunger, make love not war, justice, and social movements like inheriting his father's Civil Rights demonstration. Author *wonders* if about himself singing social change and then if made depressed afterward to prevent further singing away from his own sibling family, particularly for sans presence of parents pre-five and later extremes. Gregg felt Royal while 6 years old in initiating, supervising and overseeing a performance review of his dad the minister. This non-sick, good feeling was only during one moment while sitting in our church foyer when watching his father, his dad's associate pastor, and the choir director and full complement walk ceremoniously into worship service.

Later at Chico State University, author thought he should prove a newspaper article after a Summit written by a Chicago Theologian that could be naming someone the PRS. I thought the theologian meant not anonymously and for the PRS to be a non-celebrity. An inflated ego true it seemed, and to be realist also kept author in hiding for further accomplishment based on his own past performance. In egregious behavior that was not evangelical attempts but statements critical of using needs by the Administration with an Honorary Knight DOD Cabinet Secretary, author "war gamed love" in thoughts and demonstration in business class. Author was attempting to be inseparable to Christianity in calling attention and love to Christ to non-believers among the world's people; Asian, Islander, black Islam, Jewish, or not US friends to name some of them. Best choices should we affect foreign policy and homebound issues are to make strong a Living Christianity. Matching a breathing history without the Cold War, and more peace in fewer and smaller threats of war since before 1986 as World Equation, seems to be from advocacy at the start or origin of Peace Department if truth and hope make responsible.

We always needed our professional cadre of soldiers doing the warfare for competency in holding our enemies at bay—just keeping them there until the correct undermining from television sets to Protestant Christian teaching and the like. To reach across in hopes, needs met, and love to each other and the Greater Good principle used for peace and gain and kindness to each.

Gregg was told he was "self proclaimed royalty" from Asian women looking for work support in his adult life i.e., soliciting his endorsement for election or interviewing him for employment in job development. Arguably some of the biggest American accomplishments since Beatlemania have emanated from author's Mental Factory of his own expression and his at-hand cultural environment, and that is what we are trying to prove. His work is to regain intellectual property to be worth values and authentic credit to origin where the entrepreneur stood, sang, spoke, or scribed, et al.

The Honorable title was bestowed during his election career where he was an elected school board member and to the Democratic Central

Committee while serving as Chair of the Sonoma County Mental Health Board. T.H. is not illegal and only silly to call attention not Mr., but he wasn't told how to use it—he probably pays the fines when he is innocent. He did paid career work rated modestly exceeding expectations recognized while compromised in employment for his workability and jeopardized legally. He was both (C and J above) for not much interdependency interpersonally per governing board work forced rules keeping him in drug induced coma states re his personality.

He was legislated to fail medically once or more times, and there needs to be hope to regain his products of his mind for value to him. His peers would receive a boost for his widely known advocacy and treatment. He feels sabotaged by others, directly to his biology and indirectly by withholding credit, all to block and mortally attack an innocent man and useful voice and entrepreneur. We of, by, and for the people have taken our national productivity from using him in his leading catchy thoughts, for US Presidential MOs of many Administrations, without offering him credit and comeuppance.

Fun Mentor Lasting Within
/Just a word for acknowledgements with appreciation

Thank you, Artist my Fun Mentor in hiking and football, for securing my childhood during Vietnam. I had a blast with no meaning. I wanted to solve war and run for President, and I think you may have understood that about me without me saying it. Even though quiet with 'Bug" nickname we say Nixon demonstrated after I was called that name by nothing rude from Princeton ever at me, can you tell me if my childhood was a story of usury even then at my asshole? Whatever, it became stealing and we can fix it if accurate credit is wanted by the consumers and capital supply. I learned to respect Mr. President as a man by the stories portrayed, and we need the experience viewpoints real for us, accurate for me. The juvenile delinquency you guided helped not Mom, and you deserve an acknowledgement of gratitude for me from Nixon to History Class.

When about 5 years old I played Indians once on the initial journey up Howarth Park and you said to be just real, hiking with us. Thank you. I daydreamed a lot and liked the Native Americans long for the natural environment. The dream catcher artwork I have 2 of doesn't work for me, I found other than to keep spirit in Christianity and hope to be not shafted. If not conversing about what I want, the Dreams are withheld in discrimination based on no relationship for no meaning zero money from employers and in politics. Talk about wants, wishes, and visions and dreams to people and they or we steal the right parts and leave the second most wanted behind far down the list. Chico/Sonoma designation seems to be fun, defend dreams, and still hope for better.

I learned the sources of (from whom the people are) and the profit motive doesn't credit, and is not to be rewarded truthfully with merit income except for a prayer, hope, and chances with this Book II. Designer of A Generation means nothing to people for the Capitalists who take sources for no credit, except herein are some ideas I spread in the past to try for more both money and better, real love than can be imagined. My religion will win. I explain matters in my trademark and for beyond like I believe and work for myself to advocate.

You're credited here, Friend—Go-Long-Streak, for intelligence and fun during the childhood I loved with my family, church, and others. I thank the Safe House for your Play Room and you older boys' protection of some presence during the tumultuous 70s and those shocking crimes and wars. I enjoyed the Westerns on your TV like 49ers and The Graduate on mine. It helped with Kennedy. The State will call me The Man with No Name in ballot initiative design work for mental health services where I provide critical thinking worth myself and billions of dollars. Money eventually to get along with Peace Department I stated with free standing and structured walk through and the Czar change we want.

I took too seriously my sport in Chico, and wanted Flag Football to be an Olympic Sport. Thanks for a dream to recreate with during hard ball dynamics. Lost a tooth over it, when the RA said the biggest one wins and I carried on all the time that it was my triple bitch in ideas and designs developed for profit in reform measures if necessary. Thanks for teaching me how to play in tackle blast outs and playing defensive back. We since have had Beach Volley Ball during the Games. Over the hill players and a position for the big man all to play non-violently seems lacking in respect for geographic space problems in places in Europe. I love football and enjoyed the game played at Montgomery and on our street with our brothers. The Flag Football League as an adult was good to me for playing with the team in Sonoma County.

I'm sorry for not using individual names without the other one connected by "or" between them in every telephone greeting years long past. I liked them both as best friends and didn't need to grow more understanding than usual except knowing interpersonally the other women.

Pt. Reyes and Dissociating the Hillside Strangler

(May not be accurate, but is true portrayal of the scene I was experiencing. Trailside Strangler and above were mass murderers Spring 1978, TS caught by 1984 Marin County according to someone online. Author remains a nice man who never expected good/evil extremes were to watch for.)

I enjoyed all memory of my wonderful backpacking journeys as a youth. I loved the outdoors and felt the country would always be in me, even though I may have wanted a big city career in the future.

My first backpacking trips were in the Marble Mountains and the Sierras with church groups and a friend the summers before I was entering 7th and 8th grades. My brother was on all the backpacking trips I hiked on. One time in our Annadel State Park overnights illegally off the trail, he and my older friend carried all our clothes in storage bags over the rough to not be observed by anyone all the way to the dryer back at our house. This trip rained on us and overnight it was extremely uncomfortable with water runoff beneath us too. Our 4th Member of friendship and I stayed up there lollygagging all the following day and the sun shined down on us for more nights under the sky.

Our most advanced trip was the four of us while teenagers going to a new place in the Marble Mountains. We all got together in my brother's car, drove for hours, and stayed one week. It was good practice for me at 16 years old to drive part of the way back on Interstate 5. It was a great feeling to be in the wilds hiking into wilderness and making camp from scratch. My only regret is picking up 4th Member's fishing pole and pressing a button I didn't know on the reel. As I cast the line out into a small mountain lake where our campsite was set, using it without his permission to use his fishing pole while he was sleeping, the reel flew off into the lake. The water was ice cold and I was casting up on a very big rock, with the water below too inaccessible to retrieve the reel. As Elton John sings, "Sorry is the hardest word to say." The incident blocked me up in remorse and I explained to the friend I shouldn't have grabbed his pole. A mistake was made, but I didn't say I'm sorry. This back pack trip was the last time all 4 of us were together, and we had grown up next door neighbors starting in the 60s when I was in kindergarten.

The year earlier when I was a sophomore in high school, the Gang of 4 of us went back packing over Spring break at Pt. Reyes National Seashore. We spent two nights sleeping in meadows at two places during a 3 day excursion, with about 10 miles of hiking with full pack on between the overnight camp sites and the car where we parked.

The first night was good, with trees surrounding a secluded opening on a hillside. I didn't smoke pot like they did, as I decided to quit before age sixteen. (A digression: The six times I tried pot was embarrassingly pronounced "sex" times for 6 by Gregg from language programming for those opposed to self imposed exile. I was for one Mr. Abstinence to portray later with some repute and regard. My "MARIage-do-you-JUANA" renaming of the substance trying to demonstrate loyalty was planned by me to be exactly like a bad Catholic girl from my Protestant angle, by stating "no" more times than "yes" to something rather deviously immoral. It's minor and funny to me, as long as you don't think I'm gay when I'm straight with square morals.)

Next day hiking to the nearest camp site meadow to the ocean was fun and the site was spectacular in the open sky on a bluff, steps from the Pacific Ocean. After another night with the group of guys alone in the open, I woke up and saw white-tailed antelope on the small hills overlooking us across the way from the ocean. Just the time and place to know President Kennedy was right in starting effort to preserve this area for the Golden Gate National Recreation Area, with Nixon following up when we were young, children of the 70s and aware of the 60s history.

About mid-morning I walked over toward the coast line less than 500 hundred feet and nearly fell off the cliff. Midsize shrubs were hiding the sheer drop, and the beginning of the ocean mist and winds direction were obfuscated to line of sight from land. With my lazy eye and without glasses I must have misjudged the height of the cliff as well. I broke off an edge of the cliff standing straight upright with my foot playfully causing erosion and saw the sand fall apart. I lost track of where and how far down the sand cascaded to the ocean beach below. I got on my belly and looked at the waves. They didn't seem big, crashing on the beach below. I thought I was about 6 to 8 feet high in complete misjudgment.

Maps would have been useful, which we did not purchase to carry with us. I was thinking we were in an inlet like Bodega Bay to the north many miles, permitting me to feel overconfident believing the waves were tame. I did get nervous because there was no way to come back up the cliffs if someone fell, with soft sandstone and no one to call in ear shot up and over. It would have been miles of walking with surf crashing at any place and if the beach ran out it was death, and we did not bring rope. This was just a moot point. To fall as far down as the cliff jutted upward meant a pulverizing death from impact, perhaps with scratching the walls not breaking the freefalling descent any at all.

The older friend came over to me as I sat on the edge of the cliff. I said to him it was fun to break some of the sand off the ledge. He followed suit in standing upright like I had done, freaked out, and was agitated. I pulled him back for his balance by standing back with one hand in his front ribs and one of my hands on his back as I carefully squeezed him to terra firma. I both accidentally risked him and helped save his life by assisting his precarious balance to prevent going over the cliff.

As I was sitting with butt placement on that cliff, I completely don't know the events that happened next. I never saw the perpetrators. Did imaginary gremlins come in and tell my friends to leave in anger of my carelessness at the edge of the cliff? Or did real evil befall us?

The 3 rest of the Gang of 4 got up and left hurriedly without me noticing immediately. It took awhile to untangle fishing line which I didn't know why we had there, because I didn't think we were fishing like we normally almost always did not. I ran a different trail back toward the car and eventually home. I ran alone and I thought at the time I was with my friends instead of apparitions. On the way back in my parasympathetic part I finally realized I was alone hiking miles distant. A few people on horseback came by walking opposite my direction home toward the open camping meadow at the coast site for our previous and 2nd spot (last night). At the front of the line of equestrians was a classmate whose name I remember as I write 36 years later. As they continued past me with a cautious hello exchanged between me and the girl, I got jittery as I saw something like a metal hanger or just a branch with construction ribbon tied to mark something.

It was dangerous with horses on the not-wide trail, I thought again. I ran up off the trail at this point, up to the mountain on the right. At the top of the mountain I discovered I was standing in the midst of a stranger camp site with day packs lining the outer edges of the clearing under brush. I sat down momentarily to gain my breath and did notice there were no sleeping bags. Then I heard one horse running back toward the parking lot on the trail I had broken off from, while I was over the crest of the mountain and did not see the single horse. For the thin right of way I was on when I greeted the horsemen, I was right about danger on the trail made only for horses. In my current repast did the horseman see danger where we just had camped? Did he want to run me over to trample me to death with the horsemen blaming me for what he saw? Was the campsite extreme for ruining his day with a bloody carnage at an attempted massacre of us Gang of 4 at the scene of our nice boy campsite? I was innocent, and just had to go on with thoughts of vigilante injustice and simple teasing for being awkward at the cliff. I continued with my running carrying my backpack, with sleeping bag and all my gear, on down the other, opposite side of the mountain.

After some time I breached a return trail. It was the same trail on the way to the first secluded meadow camp site, before the fork in the trail some miles back. I hiked the rest of the way more comfortable and relaxed in thinking I would have a ride home which was 60 miles away on curvy country back roads and too far to hike, supplies notwithstanding.

When I got to the parking lot next to the Ranger Station I saw my brother's car parked and waiting for me. Room for my pack and sleeping bag in his trunk, and I didn't see anybody in the back seat. We were quiet on the drive home to Sonoma.

Looking back it could have been a police car that didn't look like that to me at the time neither does it seem like anything other than my brother's car for my memory today. My mind is running on with a forgotten nawing threat, like chewing on my nerves. I was lately writing a journal for this one experience in the process of re-memory and repast to recovery. I thought of my Sister's visit 1 1/2 years ago to the Lighthouse at Pt. Reyes and began recollecting my wonderful camp experience before writing this. With briefly walking with few females who were sister and mother, I saw that the cliffs near there were very high, like 300 feet high all around. I began to wonder about the incident of my beloved hiking spot decades ago and the people I was having fun with. I had a strong strange feeling, and now I don't want to go back without gun support and Sheriff's counselor for a date having thought dangerously since my sisters' vacation.

Before I left for the Pt. Reyes back pack trip, I read in the San Francisco Chronicle about several killings on Mt. Tamalpais by the Hillside Strangler(a 2nd separate mass killer was Trailside Strangler). It's way over there yet still at the heart of Marin County. The suspects were more than one person in the paper for each murder in these hills, and the murders were grizzly and unsolved. Next to the article was a piece on Charles Manson. When I read the news, I placed in my mind the HS was in some LA ravine. I knew nothing about crime, and heard just that Manson wanted to start a social revolution with the crime he was charged with.

Now he's in Vacaville detention facility for medical punishment/incarceration for 10 years longer ago than the pack trip.

It never occurred to me the Hillside Strangler was around alive then or even now, and those packs I saw while alone on an off trail mountaintop could have been his victims' or of just one of a team doing the killings for school Marin pride. I didn't remember the evil parts as real, or even if it was some hoax for hazing, or if the resting spot was to encourage clean up of the mountains, or they were a justice class project like Berkeley's stupid. I didn't see my friends and family leave the spectacular camp site that one day in the 70s to make events suspicious in memory, like fishing line at the murder sites of the women hikers in the articles. When writing the journal, things came to the forehead and I don't know if I said to trouble right there to no one in my vision, "It can never happen to us. We're football players. I'm nice. I'm not naïve. I don't know my family or friends bracadero." It may have been a mantra I had in my mind to say to back country murderers, and I did not remember those words until my journaling a year after visiting the Light House further up Drakes Bay when my sister visited. The mantra makes for sketchy truth to me in my recall. Why punish me for a lifetime without words present in a trial if that's what you in the court did wrongly to me a few years later when I was enrolled at SRJC? Withhold condemnation judgment where we don't know what's appropriate behavior or in questionable calls of truth and grace where the suggested MH System victim is getting poisoned at masturbation correction time, similar.

I just don't know the images. I am nice in kindness ideology belief, nonviolent by creed, a philosopher of peace and religion, tough in a way though no longer work routines, and compassionate in not wanting suffering.

I didn't like a military life to be a college to apply for and didn't at all want to join The Service for viewing a clip on TV about chemical war fare to defend against on the battle field. If this excursion of ours was the last of the HS, perhaps I did belong in a military draft in a misguided attempt for a Peace Building Division from my hometown in California. With me just saying in dissociated recall that by bringing home my men alive, scoundrels who don't believe Pt. Reyes means hope will think again. I was just not like the military in personal structure in him neither was I not trying to undermine well our business practices meaning world out far away.

I feel ironic about "virgin test subject" by people not liking me at the start of my illnesses and some who are currently. Making me suffer for too much morality, blinding someone too good who discussed politics and religion for win/win peace negotiations and efforts, and maiming my biology is evil effects to a larking lad and man who does it good. Hurting from a social discrimination that harmed my income and withholding justice to this American and denying his owning invention property and curtailing employment to a wife is wrong to do to me, who is Knight from Nebraska, Prince from Santa Rosa.

Author suggests he himself is the long time newbie who proclaims himself Virgin de la Santa Rosa for a calendar holiday worth together ship on anniversary of my birth. Take my Holiday to call someone for verbal recognition of relation like grandfather or cousin. Make one or several school age friends better known from the past and going into the new school year. Young and old people are to invite someone into the home for a soft beverage of any kind to socialize and introduce each other over the brief relationship of the annual holiday named Virgin de la Santa Rosa aka Gregg Jann Interactive Peace Day. For adults coffee or plain refrigerated water is refreshing enough and no food is necessary to cut awkward e expenses. Strategize conversation to open connections for a wider world to reach.

Chapter 6

Exploring Awareness Foreign

September 2011

Sun SS, one lady in Russia

[Thank you for writing. I appreciate you stepping in at a time like this. My father's dying does mean a test. There are church missionaries in parts of Russia and its former parts, so I'm hoping for the best in connections. No one ever expressed decency I've been or an encouragement I needed in a kind way like I wanted for me to meet and have my best luck. Ministers make mean fathers, and both parents are a harsh upbringing in the methods I was self made. I played royalty out of this family way of not emotionally supporting each other, worth a military intentional upbringing. I walk around not knowing if I will ever know if I was poisoned with certainty by anyone, space program to bear wrestling. The legend I am that was suppressed, and I didn't tell my father we cremated weeks ago any story except a consumer stated I was electrocuted. I told Dad work, Maslow, some reforms, and he told me we had a lot of fun. I loved him. The subway accident must have made the news, and getting famous without knowing it is worth something isn't it? So many economic bad raping angles that I was not knowing about, and your Russian protectors not a worry as "it is honor wins the war." Vanity bears repeating the IP one.]

Here are some basics about me before the kind of information that I should read from you soon. I recently turned past 51/50 bellwether years old. I have never been married and have no children. I live in a one bedroom apartment in my hometown's downtown. My housing is in the inner city section of about 12 square blocks in a city of 175,000 in population. The whole city is the biggest in the county, surrounded by small hills near the Pacific Ocean. Santa Rosa is 60 minutes from San Francisco by car without traffic just touching the Wine Country. I want a Luther Burbank generational saint's difference for my wife/spouse/partner/girlfriends in Charles Schulz Peanut's land where I can make it as important as a town founder. That is if breaks have it my way because the Intellectual Property occurrences happened but the credit needs to reach me dollars to come.

I love nature, walking, and try to match both as often as I can. [I don't go to the park as nearly as much as I did in the past. I'm hurt by a corrupt doctor's office when I was working on peer counseling as a professionally licensed field. It's like some kind of Irish catholic ass whole launching mortar fire on his Protestant editorialist journalist.] I used to walk 5 times a week about 4 miles each time for exercise. I have not been as faithful to my regimen recently as I used to be and have gained about 5 pounds since my birthday. Gotta stop that eating!! I like rock and roll music and sports. Mostly I like American football and used to play football as a running back and defensive back in junior high and high school days. Long ago but I won awards, had glory, and heard the crowd in the stands cheer wildly for me as I scored touchdowns and ran long plays. Just good times on the gridiron from my youth fuel my dreams at night. I like professional baseball as well, and some like of basketball.

I like animals, reading, news on TV and in newspapers, and the news I glimpse at on the web. I also will like comedies on TV, with movies and plays at the theater. I sometimes think I do social marketing pretty good. I stay active in politics by participating in a monthly dinner by selling the drink tickets like a bartender at a political club. It's kind of a funny meal when I am a former President of the political club and it's a real night out for me. I'm completely lonely except for my high Maslow which can't be joyfully happy without socially in love interpersonal connections interaction with women friends in person. My pride has been my publicly elected career as a school board official for elementary grades kindergarten through 8th grade. I am dedicated to children, the future, and wish for world peace to come to all nations. I applied myself hard in a union fight and became overexertion credit as a trucker salesman, counselor. I have dreams and ambitions about owning a foreign policy with me being the famous signature on a peace treaty. Sometimes peace isn't so popular when our country was attacked, so I keep my support trudging on to an end game of love for me and others.

Lots of writing, which is something I think I do more than women are used to. If you keep up a correspondence, you will find I write long emails. I promise to send a good picture of me in the next few emails if you write me more about yourself.

'till you write me again

11/13/11

Sun SS, one lady in Russia

Good morning my time

Nice letter I read from you.

I haven't written often because I haven't been feeling up to myself. I've been doing some head-banging letters to my IP lawyer and the Congresswoman staff here nearby.

I'm working on something to notice, unless discriminated. I feel ignored and that people are treating me as inhuman and that I'm being denied credit. This may change if I get what is offered to my accomplishment and story of peace and leadership.

As you know our country is at war. I wonder if I was recognized properly and with wishful thinking we would have a solution to ending this battle the US is in. I also think our Russia/USA standoff and rivalry can come to a peaceful end when I get more power and recognition.

Last Friday I sent emails to my IP attorney stating someone I think I am. Last Thursday I emailed Congress a request for documentation officially of my beliefs that were acted on from me unauthorized or unknown for money and wanted by me. Late Friday I called the White House and followed up with email to the President as well at 11:12pm Pacific Time zone. Sounds like I'm a community activist to you, but these plans of mine are worth a lot of a reward.

I always thought I was important. People may not always agree, particularly my family because I grew up the youngest one. That is why I say I need luck from the real and valuable thinking I have accomplished.

Not just that I think I can mature as a Capitalist/Protestant Religious Symbol, but IP I have done is valuable and hasn't been recognized since college if that. If I get lucky, I will live well and travel.

Even though my IP is real and some of it recognized as mine, this is a weird letter because people are stealing my dreams for their own profit and with their un-American morals opposing my grander ones.

ps. Read my web site? You mentioned you were "grateful" and that is the current theme on my blog. I wonder if you read it, and please tell me yes or no.

November 2011

Sun SS, one lady in Russia

Exciting for you to start your new job!! I'm glad you wrote me so I could share in the good news you are having. I appreciate you for finding work so quickly after leaving the dance and music job.

I've had a long time between jobs in the past. The way it is in America is that things take time when one is unemployed. No employer is required to hire someone. When a worker is forced out of work, the job search is all on him. He has to read the newspapers and internet to look for want ads. Sometimes it's good to drop in at an employer and ask for a job application, particularly at retail stores. Interviews are grueling, and are not offered to everyone looking for work.

Our economy has been bad in the last 3 years, now finally improving. The economic leading indicators got worse, and these indicators are things for example new home sales, unemployment statistics, and probably things like bank interest rates. Is Russia in a slump that is reported, like a recession or depression? Let me know about your general economy.

It's better for you that it took you just one week or two to find a new job. Good for you. I think being a nurse at a school is wonderful. It makes my friend S.S. look beautiful inside of her, to be caring for children like that.

If I understand it correctly, you want a better job in the long run. This job is temporary I think you told me. Your qualifications as a music and choreography teacher permit you to keep a high head on your shoulders, and want something that employs your talents. I think nurse is great, but I want you to be happy and realistic about your goals. Whatever you do for employment is fine with me. I'm proud of you, SS.

I'm also glad you understand you can't visit me. We need to share about our life more and then go from there. As you realize, my living conditions are NOT geared to me hooking up and getting hitched. Kind of like marriage rights were taken from me, mostly from being too poor. Mind you, there are ways I can break free of a rut I find myself in with women. I love my new apartment, and in the future after one year I can transfer my certificate to other housing. But the income required in limited to a low base, and we would be destitute and poor to have the rent subsidized. In the long run, its best I try to keep my HUD housing until I'm well paid. I can with a book.

Good news for me is that a non-profit offered me another gig to make money. I'm an educational presenter now, and I'm scheduled to do one or two presentations each month. I was trained to follow the non-profit's formula a few years ago, but never worked it. Then last Tuesday I presented with a second speaker at a hospital. I train interns and patients on mental illness using their guidelines. My own company gets advertising in that I mention my trademarked names in the presentation, being clear that I'm being sponsored by a company. My company named Jann Demystifying Affects or Jannda.com goes to schools and other places not just the web, and the non-profit goes to community places and in emergencies they have better name recognition.

Still my work output is short and not taking a lot of hours. My income stays the same. I'm taxed at a high rate for being on a benefit. But each work for pay makes me a little better off, but not as much as you think. I can get off the insurance with enough income as is righteous to my mental work if recognized truthfully to its use in society and economy.

The Native American event was held again last night like it is every year. It was balmy outside, and I walked around the square across my apartment window and listened to the drumming and watched the dancing. Kind of deep for me in what I imagined the dance was about, although I didn't ask anybody what the group intended. Probably an all saints day of the dead event, like our celebrating Halloween October 31st every year. It looked like a Rain Dance of Virgin women in white dresses. With set decorations of big heads of one banker in English Top Hat and a Pirate person or maybe a Indian female with the long hair above the stage that they use every year. The big heads signify local raping in my mind in the economy way of discriminating apropos human and teen sexual trafficking of immigrants. It looked like a protest like a demonstration against the bank or capitols, but probably just a celebration of an impoverished, underrepresented group like the guy writing you for being inhumanly chaste and pure and inventor.

Today, I went off to bible study at my regular Hang Outs group. It's a group of men from my dad's old P-church who get together and reflect on a bible passage. There are guidebooks on questions and points to consider, but we as a group each have something to share over the course of an hour. I was set loose liked sprinkled oats by my father and family on what it meant to be Protestant Christian, and I attended church worship services for my bible teachings. I did not get exactly correct on some important points and I don't believe in certain passages in the bible. But now I can say I'm more biblical and have more of a foundation in my faith. I'm happy for the group to practice in my life.

Take care, SS. I'm looking forward to your next letter when you have the time to write.

Prominent Public University/College of Foreign Languages
Non-personal to Professor:

After I had a phone conversation with a nearby college Social and Behavior Sciences PhD Chair, I was told to contact you by your Coordinator Amy.

Nearing the publication of my 2nd book on origins of American ledger domain due to Gregg Jann worth economy and a change for lawyers, I made up an award that may interest you in endorsing, sponsoring, or approving with input on a better name for the award I invented at the US copyright office. I am notable in Mental Health Services and a 2 time degreed person from 2 separate California State Universities in business economics and management science. I am a reformer of an authoritarian system that is Mental Health while as an employed Group Home Counselor, union community activist, and state wide advocate all the while being a consumer at threat of medicine consequences and chemical punishments akin to the Soviet Union. Currently I own a company trademarked as Jann Demystifying Affects in mental health services and I do some educational presentations on mental illness for an employed association.

It is not facetious to try for recognition as a Russian Aleksandr Solzenitsyn award as a non-English major, but a wish for university distinguished awards and reward of success to support Gregg Jann for my word-smithing ability to make an international treaty encouraging peace through medical understanding not to punish un-Americanisms of disliked behavior. I need Russian program acknowledgment from Universities like yours at to gain goals of making inroads to peace from my book titled A Jann Plan: Creative Origins Advocacy.

It is in this book where I reveal who named the AIDS acronym, the start of the internet code used in the addresses, the tax legislation of the MHSA passed by ballot in 2004, and music "larking" worth new credits all the above by Gregg Jann. A potential war definition change for stealing too much from the one with the final straw a virgin movie possibly taken by either my elected trustee years' school superintendent or by my 70s draft card older brother as the two people I told my Hollywood to besides the gaming table at Tahoe Harrah's.

I want a university award for reform to gain appropriate credit that is denied in our mental health system, the example of authoritarian ways of poison and ignoring humanity in need as a consumer and productive citizen.

You are the first professor I wrote. With your acknowledgement and assistance, I think I can help foreign relations and continue to win awards in for my health, and for the fields of medicine, peace, even economics. My 2nd book includes a suggestion for a CA ballot initiative Teach Peace and Creative Accountability written like a school board member I was formerly at Piner-Olivet USD as proposed in A Jann Plan: Creative Origins Advocacy.

My copyright application is closed albeit the certificate for Chapter 5 is in the mail with the first 4 chapters on hand. I have a great, commercial pseudonym officially that I can use on the cover that shows I contributed to Presidential works and speeches since the Reagan era.

Please accept my interests where I can try for win-win results for you to gain something from considering the Authoritarian Reform Award as a critical thinking prize in writing throughout my career. I added to a peer counseling perspective and de-stigmatization efforts in writing the first book.

I look forward to hearing from you in response. I plan on following up next week or two if you have any interest, even just to gain a quote after looking at my manuscript.

German and Russian Languages Department
Most Prominent Public University System

April 8, 2014

Same Professor,

I am following up a prior email requesting your department's "endorsing, sponsoring, or approving with input on a better name" an award I made up at the US copy right office. The work of etymology, inventions and song larking, all the while reforming the authoritarian mental health system is worth significant respect similar to my It List presence. My book received the final copy right certificate. I want a Russian themed award on reformers who could write from the beloved University, and I'm sure San Francisco wants my AIDS naming too and if they could do me reward in safety and well off I appreciate the kindness I meant with my lifetime dedication to Peace Department however strange that sounds to Finance-(crudity).

I haven't read Mr. S and misspelled his name when I "bet" I would win an award named like him and haven't been sent a fine notice from Washington, DC or his family. A woman at Santa Rosa Junior College, I don't know who she is, told me to not name the award I was working on after Aleksandr Solzhenitsyn. I am concerned about his family and the Russian culture in using a writer's name unauthorized, as well as looking less original when I only knew he emigrated to America as a Gulag reformer learned in my 9th grade World History class or was this only current events in my reading the San Francisco Chronicle? I didn't even know he won a Nobel Prize and was surprised he won the same year as Nixon. We in America do have medicine punishments and that is trying to be corrected in my career at Jann Demystifying Affects(tm), my current book, and in my elected person hood doing employment as an insider in social rehab counseling for 10 years. I intended to correct medical punishments and my first college and job recommendation was the Executive Director of the Sonoma County Medical Association and a memo to this agency in current times is in my book up for publication. It's of interest to your university in San Francisco.

I'm glad I attended then transferred from the Santa Rosa Junior College taking engineering and computer science graduating. I asked my physics instructor about Helen Caldecott for her film on Physicians for Social Responsibility and she was later nominated for a Nobel Prize I believe. Then I graduated from the two state universities with manager job in between. My first book Bettering the World states what I said that made it to then Vice President Bush during the Republican convention for his acceptance speech to set him apart from the Reagan era. In 1982, I was stranded in Chico my first Thanksgiving when the dorms were locked and Greyhound went out of business due to Reagan. I went to a friend's house like a homeless shelter and spoke detailed description of The Monkey One (title?) film made without credit to me and wrote a published editorial commentary this college weekend. In a positive direction telling you, Professor, I am working for an award for A Jann Plan: Creative Origins Advocacy which can help us with authenticity in our economy.

I may have had a part in nominating Al Gore and then Barak Obama into Nobel awards, and have done work too un-credited from a life in hiding from being first and original with the AIDS name and acronym from a newspaper magazine in 1982. President's policy/speechmaking of The AIDS speech, "Tear Down This Wall" complete with pounding fist, and Republican hard line Civil Rights apology in underwear are my speech writing with not yet crediting. This type of acknowledgement and recognition of my accomplishments that took hold in other people doing them, and getting women and voters to like me greatly can be helped by the university system of nicer people than the life I have been avoiding.

I have never been in jail or hospitalized or otherwise institutionalized. Last email had writing errors because I wrote it quickly under time constraints at the Sonoma County public library, where I find myself. I am an example of accomplishment in economics not recognized, Character Ed for children, and present on mental illness topics on special request or for a non-profit, and provide consulting on advocacy and writing from Jann DA, which is my sole proprietorship licensed in Health Services.

Are you interested in such a crediting award for reformers who could write? Would Psychology do an award like this, or is such an award too controversial for their students like I think it is?

Only Family Not Merely So Love

Family and Friends

Not to exclude or rule out a family member for too much overwork habitually, disability methods, and unfriendly spouses requires a break sometimes in close relations. When down or feeling great in success, times are for sharing with family. A goal is to keep visiting wherever you are, from tourist homesteading to hotels in origin places with disliked peers.

Toward the end of life like in retirements is when time to make up relations is there, after the squandered youth years. Prioritize and spend budgets for intentional visits together.

Keep a good attitude toward the younger social scene if you haven't married and want to be. Look for not sex, money, and even drugs for honored singles. Keeping morals worth Santa Rosa Burbank generational differences (without much carousing) takes persuasion selling of oneself to keep your outlook looking positive for a partner. New relations goals don't inhibit or exclude the set up of original family togetherness.

Find "Who" for Modern Word Choices

<u>Property Rights and Ethics</u>

Etymology is the study of the origin and history of words. Like Greek communism intakes an individual's larking talent and falsely attributes American words in agreement counter to individualism and profit. Nationalization is government taking of private property. Ask "who?" about many of our Generation's beloved word-smithing from AIDS to the internet starting linchpin to legislation in politics and for Hollywood titles and descriptions creativity.

American ledger-domain and US Economy needs rightful credit authentic to the larking source, whether he has a performance contract or not while stolen. His words by voice or print adopted from small, local places taken to afar famous needs money and recognition to the start for truth to origin. An ethic of "Pennies from Heaven" to "Pass it On" is positive attitude if Christian suffering for spreading grace and beauty while down. Origin Larks do not to be without reward else by thefts and un-crediting which evil men do.

Management Feedback Origin Hitting Snags

<u>Advocacy</u>

Being known by an American Motherhood as "calling the shots" since childhood permits playing a "Royalist" naming Duke and Duchess of Cambridge in spirit from the elected states of USA. Asking professional or professor for social favor to add to an alumni, business person, or student-rights enterpriser for win-win gainful influence worth money value and property and women to the recipient is not recognized here on the mainland. Earned distinguished awards newly founded and named after reformers who could write is a short coming of "screw you" systems like "nothing to you" political power and envy of the GOP. It's good and cooperative to know both ends can better themselves by inclusive processing of creative-type entrepreneur endeavor improving freedom and economy by understanding origins gainfully and improvement forgiveness socially for change agents.

Being a child/student while proposing on the playgrounds of Village School for interactive sports and games that required quote "management feedback" while that youth to communicate participation upon varied activities is perhaps the origin of this dialog. The State University teaching of feedback loop maps in behavioral sciences like sociology and psychology and the term "management feedback" in my business college text book on management were later read by author of this web site while in University. It's great to be taught what was spoken before while a youth leading an original on in wonder for thinking or encouragement true he is to continue influencing America and philosophy.

Am I thinking too much? I wasn't taught feedback when I first stated this and the only person who said this to me was in a bar by a musician friend while adjusting his microphone after 21. A example of a musician's feedback in electronic cacophony.

Also using psychology, I asked for no feedback to not nourish me in a Saint's method of recovery originally. Like Gulliver's travels where the miniature people tied him up behind his back, the ropes were my emotional dungeon in pulling out my feelings and passion in people ignoring me. It kept me weak during 9/11 and consumer leader locally has a smile today.

I didn't use management feedback at work in exploring effectively, both as Assistant Manager much and as line staff negotiating the first union contract. It was a qualification that I believe went unrecognized by preventing verbal assaults requiring extensive memory, footwork to the end game supervisor, and composure where I was band aided mentally by medicine. Responding to on-the-spot needs was done in my work life all places, but not references to legal contracts some I wrote while union negotiating potential or actual litigation like it's a good idea to limit comments as a professional.

Is this Original, or just different ways of talent? Using work habits is wrongful to deeply judge a man's character except in things like in ordinary income by his wife to be and usual labor pay schedules. Adding to the star creator is where the USA needs to go both socially and monetary. By the way it is not the biological parent that we reward nor is the teacher a lot. Neither should there be "UNMONEY" for too famous larks or achievements or parents or teachers. Mother is for "royalty" to recognize outside of family. Family wants and wishes do not belong on the job except in emergencies or senior age and is not the social support we need to keep performing good habits. Larking like we've said is a hard creative process.

We are to learn to reward with merit pay the achieving creator and the creative accomplishment in our status quo where ever the organization or person leader is now added to by the achieving origin point sources. Tell me with information, story, and show me the money size of all of Missoula if word smithing by author was used famously like we think it is.

Starting Stars Appear Targets of Misanthropy

Prevention and Health

A child started in my back yard "check in" with psychology with his head butt to sister's heart nearly 1/2 century ago. To him, he was trying for wisdom gain from words of her feelings and activity. The "Check In" tool currently directs therapy sessions from that selfless youngster who didn't ask money from his clergyman-dad. Now he's a professional wordsmith with health business license with some industry experience and not yet paid for necessary influences.

"Check in" as a mental health status meeting or nicely applied to the person-part prevalence does not have a recorded origin at my finger tips.

Kindness intent for trusted connecting, whether to stabilize or support thoughts, feelings, acts, and/or perceptions; started "check in' practices in the industry first and originally used by me for communication. The one time use worked in my memory by not over exploitation concerns of my creative product from watered stock in my mind (not outward) and is now written with ownership.

Emotionally Investing for Freedom

Prevention and Health

I know sometimes I refer to struggling through adversity makes one more satisfied with his life journey once reaching wellness. The weekend cost money to lose an appearance fee on inner conflict on non-tangential observations. I hope to make a difference everywhere I was last weekend. Wear Nancy Kerrigan white for rougher innocence first we meet.

Investing in a world view with more freedom to the world's people takes good news at Olympics and life nearby. Hearing "artificial entities" in community organizing against corporate personhood and encouraging political speech not equal to money makes a worry about persons with disabled stigma.

Trying to eradicate Malaria with a financial contribution to Methodist fundraising emanates a feeling of St Valentines. Viewing "Russian Glory" by young women is culture of that rival, and did no recovery for a Scarlett Letter for no sin and no crime and a lost Elvis coat accidentally left behind.

Sochi Olympics and Beatlemania

Homeland into Foreign Policy

Some good news finally came in after a passion and emotional dungeon that is my "GIGO Method" on mental health recovery. This method can block news of the world except de facto drug and alcohol scuttlebutt. Preventing worldliness in more cosmopolitan environs of the Wine Country, USA can harm a person's standing in the community if he carries class somewhere in his background, i.e. college degrees, professions in his family, or upper middle class tastes in things near San Francisco.

Finally learning Beatlemania arrived in the US in 1964 on February 7. When did "I Want to Hold Your Hand" get taken and did it come from "Eyiou" in the heartland? 2) The Russian flag changed from the Hammer and Sickle of communism back in the 90s. Healing takes time, and is a weird thing to do within politics. Shaman-stories, -accomplishments, and -innovations are banned by the Military Academies in the US President and in our economic careers for related success, but not for USA in people.

Song Origin: "I Want to Know What Love Is"

Property Rights and Ethics
Reviews and Entertainment

I saw Foreigner live, a great rock act of British and Americans, locally last November 7th. I first heard this group 1977 on the radio.

The Chorus performance were student singers, noted from the same high school I graduated with the original recording Chorus not far from the other coast houses we also lived. I completely thought back to one struggle in my lifetime of aloneness running uncharted over "mountains I must climb." The lead singer and the flood lights with audience variances in standing set the scene up. I more than related to the night's show and felt satisfied and challenging for my credits.

I wailed singing FO in the 70s, "I want to know what love is. I want you to show me" and some of the other lines while running over mountains away from hazy indescribable bad trespassing and harm bearing scenes. Feeling complete with surefire memory of a single horseman running back in the valley below at my only un-hiding spot where evidence meant murder.

While often enjoying nature, playing sports, studying in and out of school, working teenage employment, perhaps even family; I would be in trances noticed by a trained singer particularly. I repeated over and over my own F.O. song lyrics, in full part. These were different trances than the manic states of hard rock listening to my stereo for years.

Composers or merely unethical "Communicative Facilitators" played out my FO Larking talent without my awareness to take this song without me in any permission to writ large in dishonest credits the song larking I performed used by Foreigner, others who seem mainly British. The power of radio play on me resulted lying to me since the 70s, (60s?) as strong as Fascism on origin point and source perspective design for several singing legends for much of the 80s rock era and still performed.

It was just deathly dissociative amnesia (event suppression) for harm from another country and similar to me with long indirection of nearly a lifetime to get to what is actual starts and parts and whole accurately in song. There is much else from this author/source that is theft and fraud to origin currently in entertainment, health, and computers - not to mention government functioning in their participants' stories for experience and viewpoint. Let's correct inaccurate credit, IP fraud and theft injustices and mean something about it. We may even lead with new credits worth better economy as I propose to do.

Contact Us at Jannda.com and include your name with mailing address to Jann D A/Advocate in regard to your information about crediting the origin/source viewpoint of this song by Foreigner as it exists currently and more things as mentioned above with greater accuracy if not noted. Looking for other starts and viewpoints utilized specifically so we can correct an ingenuine aspect in American commercial products of the mind.

Accomplished and too Legendary Early

Critical Thinking Fighting Suppression

Always accomplished and still legendary early feels fresh and that is author. Suppression 1)man-made 2) God fearing, has no permission to eliminate memory and feeling. It just does. Why would you do so?

Starting and living projects and stories with author's own ideas that are expressed in positions appointed, elected, or employed: sales, mental health, education; and working outside the box makes results from a leader who influences our nation.

See enough individualism that Capitalism warrants in emotionally supporting the leader or those near you for their genesis work and true historical value.

Good managers can fill a hole for the unique person of influence who may be struggling. Is the outside leader like vying for Honorary Knight for change? Author loves and does US and you better, kinder, and more understanding beyond pleasant demeanor. Are stories of him known internationally or places Sacramento?

Hope/Commemorating the Prince of Peace

Holistic Community and Permaculture

Consider the Star of David this Christmas Eve, for long lasting thoughts, deeds, and standing beyond reputation. Aim high and shoot straight, with honesty in verbal output authentic to those good wishes for others and in only residually the comeuppance you receive from good karma.

The Prince of Peace shook the world about 2000 years ago in the Holy Land. His words and miracles spread to other lands including our own America. Christmas is celebrating his birthday, and no commercial or joyous commemoration is as great a holiday for USA culture.

The Hope we have is for us to act within and for those who see to us outward, trying to gain our health and live in peace for all mankind. Let's work together emotionally, spiritually, and in tasks to deliver a wholesome feeling of good love and benevolence to our fellow men and women with our own selves included.

Renewing the Kind MInd to Fill Gaps

Holistic Community and Permaculture

It's a great opportunity to keep on learning for a lifetime, whatever the mode of inquiry or field. Whether the oratory for Sunday preaching needs more understanding for a Bible Group to participate in reading, or watching quality shows on TV on Ancient History and great Religions of the world all add to a person's inside. Thinking cap stuff can age and be broken in the chakra at the top point of the head for nearly harm done. Author was attacked by a Chinese Ambassador at CSU indirectly questioning about alternative medicine. A gap in thinking above can inspire activity, peace, and warm regard in the daily doings of the semi-retired or more pedestrian lifestyle. Spirituality and religion is more feeling, and the study here can be additional intelligence and wisdom along the paths already chosen for you. It can be great karma and a blessing to visit the museums of San Francisco and the hilltops for learning about culture and the love of beautiful people I want to be myself.

2nd Chances Out to There: US, Foreign Policy

<u>Homeland into Foreign Policy</u>

This country was founded by people coming to America for a better life. Accepting 2nd Chances and more than 2 opportunities are important. "Let me up" is an answer to greater socioeconomics starting with supports and aid forgiveness. Upward Social Mobility principle is quintessential American.

Tolerance of Recovery and adding different types of recovery will grow and develop our understanding of others, increase our personal depth, and bond us together for national character that means it. USM once hurt lives on. Reaching across wins friends among nations not as rich as ours.

Having this stronger leadership quality more pronounced throughout the country will guide us through. Appreciate each for USM, Recovery of illness and/or addictions, and mainly those understanding of others for thick talent a mile deep for the USA. It's worth US President to be the stars of recovery, of relating talent, and consistent USM advocacy. I'll accept your nomination.